Making Your Dreams Come True®

Marcia Wieder

CEO/Founder
Dream University®

Published by DreamU Publications,
110 Pacific Avenue #355, San Francisco, California 94111
Dream University – **www.DreamUniversity.com**

Originally published in earlier editions, by Greater Wisdom Publishing Corporation in 1993 and by Harmony Books in 1999.

MAKING YOUR DREAMS COME TRUE is a registered trademark of Marcia Wieder.

Printed in the United States of America

Cover design by Chris Collins, American Design Co.

Library of Congress Cataloging-in-Publication Data
Wieder, Marcia.
Making your dreams come true / by Marcia Wieder. Rev. ed.
1. Success-Psychological aspects I. Title.
BF637.S8W512 1999
158.1-DC21
99-31657

Library of Congress Control Number: 2010908462

ISBN 978-0-615-37879-4

10 9 8 7 6 5 4 3 2 1

Second Revised Edition

For All Who Dare To Dream—

And especially for Patrick, the man I love.

Acknowledgements

THANK YOU TO MY FAMILY and dear friends who love and support me and believe in my dreams. You are my core.

A very special, "I couldn't have done it without you" words of appreciation to my team and partners Angela Berg-Dallara, Patrick Wyzorksi, Lynn Hargis, Kelley Moore, Ridgley Goldsborough, Hubert Lee, Jeff & Ryan Hilton, Ken Atchity, Steven Weinberg, Erin Saxton, Chris Collins, Liana Chaouli, Michael Silvers, Cynthia Kersey, Stephen Dinan, Jack Canfield, Marci Shimoff, Deirdre Hade, Angel Evans and Sharon Cline. I also offer deep gratitude to the hundreds of Dream Coaches I've had the honor to train and certify in this work.

Mostly, thank *you* for reading this book and for spreading the word that our dreams are precious and essential. May your life be filled with love, joy and abundance.

And thank you God, for reminding me that we are all dreamers at heart, and for granting me the privilege to do this work.

Table of Contents

Foreword

**You've got to have a dream if you
want to make a dream come true.**
— RODGERS AND HAMMERSTEIN

WHAT IF YOU COULD CREATE what you want by being able to close
the gap between dreams and reality? In person and now in Making
Your Dreams Come True, Marcia Wieder shows people how to close
the gap.

As a professional speaker, Marcia's spirit and style electrifies any
room. She produces powerful results with her corporate clients and
business associates worldwide. In describing what Marcia's system does
for them, clients have commented that she produces amazing results
and re-ignites passion in the audience. After engaging with Marcia,
people who claim to have forgotten their dreams remember and "get
going" on that dream.

I first met Marcia shortly after reading books by Richard Bach and
Jane Roberts. These writings profoundly changed my life, and when I
realized they could change anyone's life, I felt compelled to share this
joy with everyone I came in contact with. Just then, I met Marcia.
Coincidence #1.

Our career paths took us in different directions, and we lost contact for some time. At the precise moment when I was in the process
of rediscovering my own true purpose and my life was again beginning
to take on an exciting new direction, Marcia called me and asked me to
read *Making Your Dreams Come True®*, and to write a foreword. I felt the

joy of the knowledge and wisdom contained in this book, and again the compulsion to help share it with everyone. Coincidence #2.

It is said that when the student is ready, the teacher will appear — and vice versa. The fact that you are reading this book is no accident. Coincidence #3.

Marianne Williamson writes that all of our choices are made either out of love or out of fear. *Making Your Dreams Come True*® also speaks to this basic truth. If you are passionate, love what you do, and spread that love through what you do, the possibilities are limitless.

There are many paths to the truth. In this book, Marcia has been able to garner truths from many sources, and has uniquely combined this knowledge in a practical and pragmatic guide to self-discovery, or better yet, rediscovery. This book provides a real basis for applying these truths, and gives us an imaginative action plan placing us on a path to realizing our greatest dreams.

I have rediscovered that I have always been at my happiest and most successful, when working with the things I love, that are exciting to me, that I feel passionate about, and in which I feel a compulsion to make a contribution. Through all my various career experiences, from being NBC's executive in charge of the original *Saturday Night Live* to becoming an Emmy award-winning producer, I have always been most successful when surrounded by, or in close proximity to, the elements of my passion.

Is it any wonder that I now find myself working as an entertainment producer in a place that started as the dream of one man; Walt Disney World, and where the vision statement of Walt Disney World Entertainment is "Dream it, Create it, Deliver it!." Coincidence #4!

With regard to all the "coincidences," the explanation "it's a coincidence" doesn't really explain anything. Coincidence merely means two or more events coinciding; the odds of which we are conditioned to believe are very highly improbable if not impossible. The power of dreams, and the power you will derive from *Making Your Dreams Come True*® will allow you to transcend the improbable and the impossible. Read the book...and then watch the coincidences!

You are about to embark on an exciting journey in a realm that perhaps you thought you couldn't do much about — making your dreams come true. Bring your hopes and highest aspirations, because *Making Your Dreams Come True*® is going to show you how to make them a part of your everyday existence. We need big dreamers at this time in the world. I'm excited for you.

— Rick Traum
Producer, Walt Disney World Entertainment

Preface

YOU ARE ABOUT TO EMBARK ON an exciting personal journey in a realm that you perhaps thought you couldn't do much about—making your dreams come true. Yes, bring your doubts, fears, and concerns, because I will help you address them, head-on. But also bring your hopes and highest aspirations, because *Making Your Dreams Come True®* is going to show you how to make them part of your everyday existence.

My life is a dream come true. In all areas of my life I'm living a life I love. This book will show you how to do the same for yourself.

This is a tried and true, tested and proven program that will take you through a step-by-step process for Making All Your Dreams Come True.

The basic formula is:

1. Get clear about what your dream is.
2. Remove the obstacles, especially the limiting beliefs, and
3. Design the simple steps to make it happen.

The essence of the formula is passion. Passion is what excites and compels you, what makes your life rich and extraordinary. This book will show you how to discover or rediscover what you're passionate about and how to bring it to all areas of your life. How does that sound?

For ten years I lived in Washington, D.C., and was president of a multi-media creative services agency managing up to fourteen employees. Although successful by many people's standards, I was not passionate about what I was doing, about how I was doing it, about the people with whom I was doing it, and about where I was doing it.

My dream was to be free—free to travel anywhere, anytime. Free to do what I wanted when I wanted, even to have my portable office be wherever I happened to be.

My dream included a magnificent view of water and mountains, clean, fresh air and a quiet, healthy environment.

My dream included partnering with creative visionaries to make an impact on the world, in addition to traveling the world in style and elegance, speaking about something inspiring.

My dream included having lots of fun, creating my work as play and living a life filled with full self-expression.

Sound outrageous?

I picked up and moved to San Francisco. When people ask why, I tell them because I was craving a beautiful view and a different kind of lifestyle, which is what matters to me now. Once committed, I climbed into my car and took a few months to visit with friends and family as I made my way west, with my fax machine and laptop in tow.

I became a successful Dream Coach®, speaker and author. During the period of a few months, I was paid to travel to Hawaii, Rome, Greece, and Indonesia, inspiring people to dream.

I've worked with thousands of people personally and professionally in some of the biggest and most wonderful companies in the world. I help them get clear about their vision, and mission, and support them as they get into action on their dreams and their lives. I founded and lead Dream University®, retreats for visionaries and big dreamers. I look and feel ten years younger, and I'm the healthiest I've ever been. I'm completely free and very happy.

It all begins with a dream. You can make your dreams come true. It all starts here. So, let's begin finding, fine tuning and achieving your dreams. I'm excited for you!

MAKING YOUR DREAMS COME TRUE

Introduction

YOU ARE HOLDING IN YOUR HANDS the definitive work on making your dreams come true, having the life you love, and living a life filled with passion; in essence, having it all. When you've finished reading this book you will know how:

> You really want your life to be,
> You can develop a dream that inspires you,
> You can look at your life with a fresh perspective, and
> You can design your environment to implement the techniques you've learned.

Beginning with the first chapter you will learn to empower yourself and believe in your ideas. Possibilities you never knew existed will emerge, and you will trust the resources in your life to help you produce amazing results in your everyday life, with greater ease.

Sound enticing?

In every chapter you will find clarity as well as the action steps that will prompt you to nod in knowing appreciation. The pages in this book will offer you methods of achieving everything you want in life. The hands-on exercises presented throughout will help serve as your personal record of everything you learned about your dreams and how to accomplish them. The Making Your Dreams Come True® Workbook will walk you through the process.

This book is written with you as its focus. You can use it as if it was a highly-paid dream coach or architect, taking you by the hand to lead you through the process of making your dreams come true. Interact fully with its pages and, when you are done, I believe you'll say, "Yes, I can make my dreams come true anytime I choose."

There is a wonderful dream story that accompanies the publishing of this book. It demonstrates exactly what I teach. You need to believe in your dream, even if it initially seems like a long shot. Find DreamTeam members, people who will support you and help make your dream happen. Finally, as you articulate your dream with passion and clarity, and demonstrate that you believe in your dream, others will get on board, and perhaps even take your dream to a whole higher level.

Years ago, I had the pleasure of meeting George Hall, Vice President for Body Wise International, a wonderful network marketing company that sells excellent nutritional supplements and believes in personal empowerment. George and I had an immediate affinity for each other, since we are both big dreamers. As a matter of fact, George is 6' 6" and a stunt pilot enthusiast. One of his dreams was to compete in acrobatic flying, which he later did. George hired me to speak at several events for Body Wise, to inspire thousands of people to take risks and go for their dreams.

One of the people in the audience was Caroll Roberson. Caroll later attended Dream University® (you'll read more about her story later) and so believed in my message that she even came back as a facilitator. Caroll became an essential member of my DreamTeam. Here's what happened.

I produced a new audio series called *Design Your Dream Life*. Caroll sent the program to her friend Lori Glasgow at KVIE – Public Broadcasting System in Sacramento, California. But Caroll didn't stop there. She was tenacious and relentless in calling Lori and urging her to listen to the program. Lori listened, loved my message and called me. She wanted to feature me in a one-hour national television special and invited me to become a partner. The magic had begun.

Then I met Jan Tilmon, a creative and brilliant woman at KVIE who helped launch the careers of the wonderful writer Leo Buscaglia and

Covert Bailey (Fit or Fat). Her vision was that my life was about to change. We agreed that we would produce a show called *Making Your Dreams Real* and I would travel all over the United Stated as part of a major fund raising drive for PBS.

There was just one thing missing. In conjunction with the audio-tapes, we needed the book. We literally had only six months to get it into the stores and we had not identified a publisher for it. I called my agent Bonnie Solow. She was concerned about the time frame, but my passion ignited her, and she made an important phone call to a woman of true vision, a really big dreamer. Patty Gift at Random House asked me to rush her my materials and in less than 24 hours, we had an amazing deal and a commitment to have this book into the stores and your hands right away.

As luck would have it, I was flying to New York the next day to present a workshop to The Gap. I swung by Random House and met my new team. The entire team was there to greet and welcome me.

I left the meeting filled with joy. I had found the perfect Dream-Team. They passed the true test of a great DreamTeam with flying colors. They love my dream, they are willing and able to make my dream theirs, and finally, and this is my favorite part, they will make my dream even bigger.

Everyone you meet serves an important role in your life. Use this book to sharpen your awareness and to find like minded big dreamers. Through this very special book, reconnect to your passion, find and create dreams that honor your heart's desire and prepare for the magic and surprises that are available to all dreamers. Count me on your DreamTeam.

CHAPTER 1

What Is a Dream?

Nothing happens unless first a dream.
— CARL SANDBURG

MOST PEOPLE THINK OF DREAMS either as some kind of unattainable fantasy, or as something they do in their sleep. Neither of those definitions are what I mean when I speak of dreams.

I define dreams as the aspirations, desires, goals, and hopes that you most want for yourself. Moreover, these are the kind of dreams you have while you are very much awake.

My formula for *Making Your Dreams Come True* is:

First
Get clear about what your dream is.

Second
Remove the obstacles, especially the limiting beliefs.

Third
Design the simple steps to make it happen.

Dream (n.), a fond hope or aspiration; (v.) to conceive of or devise.

Possibility (n.), that which may or can be, that which may or can be done, that which is capable of existing, something that is conceivable.

Beliefs (n.) What you hold to be true, your opinions and judgments.

Steps (n.) the act of moving from one place to another, to progress.

It's that simple. That's the formula for having it all—a life you love, and the time and freedom to enjoy it.

Four Key Words

The word "dreams" has long been misinterpreted, as if dreams were like puffy clouds in the sky—beautiful, but unreachable. The dictionary offers a different interpretation not only of "dreams" but of several other words that I'll be using throughout this process. Therefore, I'll start by defining some terms:

Dream - a fond hope or aspiration; to conceive of or devise.

Possibility - that which may or can be, that which may or can be done, that which is capable of existing, something that is conceivable.

Beliefs - What you hold to be true, your opinions and judgments.

Steps - the act of moving from one place to another, to progress.

It's interesting that the dictionary describes "dream" as a way to achieve your fond aspirations, which suggests possibility and hope, while most people have a sense of hopelessness and futility about their dreams. Yet, their dreams continue to live as an ember, flickering in the back of their minds. Using this book, you will learn to create clarity about what you want, and to get your dreams out of your head and into your reality.

Many of us regard "possibility" as something that's not *im*possible, although Webster tell us that possibility is something within the realm of our grasp. I used to believe that anything was possible as long as I could figure out in advance how to do it. Eventually I realized this was a limiting belief because sometimes the perfect strategy might not be immediately evident. Not having a plan all mapped out should not be the reason you don't believe something might still be able to happen. I was stopping myself from going for what I wanted, often before I even began. Now I believe that *everything is possible* as long as I believe it. It is believing in our dreams that often gives us the courage to act on them, to take the important steps froward. My life is filled with opportunities galore, many that I surely would not have encountered if I was still operating with my old belief.

WHAT IS A DREAM?

Indeed, when you open up to the potential of having what you want, you allow wonderful people and events to appear in your life. When you clarify what you're committed to having, and believe that Everything Is Possible, the results in your life will seem effortless and show up easily. Do you want greater ease in your life?

I love the dictionary definition of Possibility. It reinforces the concept that much of our lives is or can be filled with extraordinary results. Have you written this off in your life as illusionary? Are you or have you become overly realistic? Reality is an important part of the mix, but being too realistic can squelch your passion and your dreams.

Dreams belong in our homes and workplace. The ideal situation which I'll discuss in detail, is bringing more of what you love into your everyday life. Like Paul Scott, the senior vice president of Worldwide Field Operations at Lucent Technologies. Paul has a passion for fun and he demonstrates it all day and every day at work, even under times of change and pressure. Since one of his true passions is golf, he's always willing to entertain and educate important clients out on a beautiful course. And why not? He totally gets it about passion as does his exceptional and cutting edge company. Lucent Technologies hired me to design and implement a yearlong program called "The Passion Plan." They know happy people make happy employees, and happy employees produce better results.

AT&T, one of America's corporate giants, has a campaign for its employees called Ten Million Magic Moments. AT&T says, and I agree, that it's time to find a new way of speaking, thinking and doing things, which includes fun and creativity. Whether we refer to it as purpose or mission, there is an important place for vision in business too. Charles Schwab the financial giant's mission statement says, "We are the custodian of our customer's dreams." That's why they have my business.

You can start making your personal and professional dreams come true today—right now—by being clear about what a dream is, by believing in your dreams, and by taking simple steps.

What Is Your Dream?

When I listen to people as they discuss their dreams, they seem so quickly to abandon what they want. The tone is often something like, "Well it might be nice, but it probably will never happen, so why bother?" Are you simply dismissing your most heartfelt desires? Do you even know what they are?

In talking to people about what they want, I find that most of them characterize "dreams" in the same way they perceive "fantasy." That is, most people don't believe their dreams will come true unless something miraculous happens: if they win the lottery, if Mr. or Ms. Right comes along, or if their stars are aligned in the heavens.

Here is a simple and powerful distinction between a dream and a fantasy. In a dream you can design a strategy for making it happen. In a fantasy like winning the lottery, there is nothing that you can do to make sure it happens. Sure, fantasies can occur, but again, there is nothing you or I can do to ensure it.

Keep in mind, you are the one who needs to make the distinction. When I announced to friends and family that I was moving to San Francisco to become a Dream Coach, they thought this was a fantasy and were concerned about my sanity. But I believed in my dream, I could conceive of the strategy and was committed to making it happen. Therefore it was a dream, and one that did come true.

A dream can be exotic or glamorous, but it does not have to be. Your dream can be anything from spending more time with the family to growing your business. It can be to become healthier and more physically fit, or to write a book. Dreams can range from the mundane to the esoteric, and sometimes what you truly want can come as a complete surprise to you. At the end of this chapter you will find some "Real People" stories. These anecdotes are used as illustrations throughout the book. They are all true situations and they all demonstrate how the techniques I'll describe can be used in every facet of your life.

To enter into the process of achieving your dream, start with Step One, clarifying what you want. On the facing page there is a place for you to commit your dream to paper. Put into a single sentence the essence of what you're committed to having. Don't worry that you can't define all the details; they'll come as you move forward. The key is to get in touch with what you feel passionate about, what excites and motivates you. And if you don't know what your dream is, perhaps that is the main reason why you bought this book, I have two simple suggestions. One, you could write, "my dream is to have a dream" (trust me, you are not alone on this one). Or, you could start small, by writing down one small thing that you would like to have or do. Remember, a dream is simply something you want.

Write down what you want. If you can't formulate your dream yet, make something up. Start someplace. Although it may seem ridiculous now, it will often work to lead you down the right path. When you're ready to write your dream, you can apply the techniques you learn as you move through this book. Think about a time in your life when you spoke to others about an idea, and your idea turned into something more concrete. Perhaps the more you talked about your concept, the more real it became. Getting your dream out of your head, gets the ball rolling.

Everything Is Possible.

LIFE CAN BE
A DREAM COME TRUE.

Identifying Your Dream

(Example: I, Diane, will have great success in my new business while balancing my family and social life.)*

I, _____, have the following dream:

_____

_____

_____

* Balance, in some form, is the most common dream people have described when working with me.

What Are Your Expectations?

What do you expect to have when you've finished this book? Perhaps you're looking for a blueprint to get you from where you are to where you want to be. Maybe you're seeking a strategy or steps that will divide the work of reaching your dreams into specific areas of concentration.

You can turn this book into an action plan for making your dreams come true by deciding now what you intend to have by the time you've finished reading it. My goal is that you fulfill your dreams as you complete the book; if that's not your goal, too, you may want to put the book down now, and think about why you bought it in the first place.

The process of defining your expectations and getting your dream out of your head and into reality can follow these steps:

Think about what you want;

Visualize what you want;

Write down what you want and read it aloud to yourself;

Speak about what you want, and share it with others;

Listen to yourself, and for opportunities in the world to make your dreams come true;

Be your dream, actually live it;

Do what you want to do, so that you can have what you want to have.

Get up and get going. As Nike says, "Just do it."

Start to act the part right now. If your dream is to run a dude ranch, the first thing you might do is buy boots and a cowboy hat, and have fun wearing them around the house. I know it's a small step, and to your rational mind it may even seem a little silly, but you have to start wherever you can. This becomes your point of access or port of entry. Besides, if your dream is to some day golf in the Masters Tournament, you have to get out, practice, and play now.

That first step may be enough for you right now. Perhaps you decide that you want to be in greater action toward your dream, or that you want your dream to come true in its entirety by the end of this book. It's all up to you. Have a sense of humor and "play" with it; it doesn't need to be hard work. Enjoy the process.

The techniques await you. Don't sit back to see how it unfolds; it *won't* happen unless you interact with the process. Let this book make a difference in your life; use it to pull you forward so you can get what you want. Start now.

Real People: Larry

Larry wanted to double his business within the next calendar year without burning himself out. His goal was reasonable; in fact, it's done all the time. Larry came to me because he didn't know how to accomplish it and he felt that something was in his way. He just couldn't quite put his finger on what it was.

MY GOAL IS THAT YOU
FULFILL YOUR DREAMS
AS YOU COMPLETE THIS BOOK.

I told Larry that we'd start the process of making his dream come true by getting in touch with what he's passionate about. Larry balked. "Wait a minute," he said. "I don't want to examine my whole life, I just want to know how to double my business."

I said, "Larry, you have to trust the process." He'd heard these words before.

What Larry discovered by following my approach was that having powerful partnerships and intimate relationships had been driving forces throughout his life; that's what excited him. Although he "knew" this subconsciously, actually articulating it gave him a real boost of energy. He was excited about making this part of his business goal.

When he realized the passion he felt about creating powerful partnerships, Larry understood that he needed to learn how to develop associations with anyone at any time and that this would be the secret to his success.

As we continued to probe, Larry became aware that, by holding onto old beliefs that no longer served his needs; he was limiting his potential to create partnerships. For example, he had developed the habit of not "revealing his playing cards," he feared taking the "wrong" kind of people into his confidence, he worried that others wouldn't uphold their end of a bargain, or that they didn't have the "right" address or the "best" credentials to be his partner. He eliminated wonderful potential partners before ever giving them a chance. Together, we removed the obstacles, the limiting beliefs that were in Larry's way. This had a huge impact and immediately freed him up to dream big.

Trust the process
of making your dreams come true.

Once clear about what made him feel passionate and with his limiting beliefs out of the way, Larry made a conscious commitment to develop partnerships with anyone that he chose. Now he's excited about living his life, not just about doubling his business.

Passion is the access to power; when Larry got in touch with his passion, he developed the power to take the first step toward his dream. Now he has more than two dozen strategic partnerships with associates, friends, agents, even competitors, all of whom are helping him achieve his goal of doubling his business. Larry understands passion is as a component in the formula for success and that people are central part of his passion.

Real People: Nancy

Nancy had been successful on Wall Street, making a six-figure salary. Now she was starting a whole new life: she was simultaneously pregnant with her first child, and leaving the world of stocks and bonds to start a new business. She was absolutely committed to her dream of having quality personal time with her friends and family, while developing and building a new business. She was determined to have a balanced life.

A successful person is often also an overcommitted person, and Nancy fit the description. She was aware that she had designed so much into her life that there wasn't room to create anything new. Therefore, we began by cleaning out the clutter. We moved things out of the way, consolidated, organized, and created space, not just physically but emotionally, mentally, and spiritually. Finally, Nancy had *room* to design a whole new future, and she began to live her dream by making deliberate choices, not merely responding to whatever life threw her way.

Then we designed the strategies for her to achieve her dream. There were specific marketing and sales techniques for growing the business, but there were also strategies for enjoying her pregnancy and having quality time with her husband.

Get in touch with your passion.

Wherever possible we doubled up on strategies, to allow Nancy more time. For example, one tactic that permitted Nancy simultaneously to enjoy her pregnancy and to have quality time with her mate was to take a daily walk with her husband. Later, we turned this technique into a project with the goal of walking two hundred miles before the baby was born. This project supported Nancy's needs for a healthy body and baby, for exercise and relaxation, and for time with her spouse. Do you need to clear away some clutter, in order to make some serious space for your dreams? You'll learn more about projects, strategies, and steps as you read on.

Real People: Ilene

Ilene was once a professional dancer, studying under Alvin Ailey. As a sideline, she founded a small dance company while working at a full-time job. Her dream was to quit her job, to become the full-time executive director of her dance company, and to do it within 30 days.

She had many beliefs and fears that were stopping her from achieving her dream. Ilene and I worked intensely through a long session to get clear about her dream and to remove the self-imposed limits that prevented her from reaching it. As we grappled with these issues, she began to share her dream, expressing her hopes about making it happen. She was committed to finding people who would help her. Ilene was surprised and delighted to find that going through the process made her see the dream as bigger than her current reality; this change of perception made her more committed to having the dream than to remaining in the *status quo*.

Live your dream by making

deliberate choices,

not just responding

to whatever life throws your way.

One of Ilene's concerns had been how she would finance her new venture and support herself at the same time. Together, we were able to design a plan that enabled her to resign her full-time position and still pay her bills. One of the ways we did that was by defining a skill—grant proposal writing—that Ilene could use as a freelancer. Once she realized she didn't need to be a salaried employee, she turned her current employer into her client, and she generated $25,000 of income for herself within the first few weeks after she was on her own. Originally Ilene thought that her current employer was the one person who would not support her dream. This was a limiting belief that she uncovered and removed.

Once Ilene knew how she would pay the rent, she turned her attention to her new venture. She assembled a board, scheduled recitals, and got into action living her dream. She did not have the budget to fulfill this dream, but her passion and dream, also known as 'sweat equity," made it happen. The first major performance of Ilene's dance company, which I'm pleased to say I attended, was offered to an audience of more than 200 people.

Commit to your dream.

Real People: George

At one time George had been severely overweight. Through great effort and perseverance, he had trimmed down, and he was feeling great about being healthy. Now his dream was to stay physically fit, but he was having trouble getting himself motivated to go to the gym three times a week.

In exploring George's life we discovered that his passion was to live life as an adventure. To George, that meant trying new things, seeking new challenges—in short, George hated feeling bored.

Out of his enthusiasm for testing himself in new situations, George designed a project that would allow him to fulfill his dream adventurously. The project he took on was to train for a triathlon. The venture had George feeling turned on, lit up, passionate, and he had no difficulty getting to the gym with regularity. He even hired a coach to help him break through any limitations. The more George pushed himself beyond where he was, the more passionate he became. This is inherent in his Purpose, to live life as an adventure.

Here's just a quick note for you. If your dream is to be in great shape without having to go to the gym, this need not be considered a fantasy. My strategy for exercising without daily visits to the gym included taking up skiing and roller blading (with lots of appropriate padding) at the age of 40.

Make the dream bigger
than your current reality.

Real People: The Carters

The Carters are a married couple who owned a computer store in a fancy shopping center. Like many people, their dream was to have financial freedom while having the time to enjoy each other. After a session with me, the Carters realized that maintaining their current business was working against achieving their dream. The massive overhead in their upscale setting was eroding their profits, and the retail nature of their establishment meant that they were always "on call" when the store was open. They needed more flexibility, and they recognized that, to get it, they would have to close the store and change to a new business. They considered this a daring and a very scary move.

One of the best aspects of the techniques used in this book is that they can be used to create balance; after all, part of having it all is having the time to enjoy it. The Carters didn't know at first that their dream included closing down their store; it only became clear during the process. They were passionate both about being in business and about having time for each other, but their passion did not include owning a retail operation. Once they were committed to realizing their passion, they were ready to get into action toward having their dream. You will see as their story continues later in this book that they did it in record time.

Allow yourself to get lit up,

turned on,

and really passionate

about your dream.

CHAPTER 2

The Passion Pyramid

Passion is the access to power.

— MARCIA WIEDER

MY TECHNIQUES FOR MAKING your dreams come true have several advantages over other approaches. One of the benefits is that you don't have to choose having your dream in one area of your life over getting what you want in others.

I often hear people lament that they could have what they want if they gave up other things, or that they must work endless, tedious hours to earn the kind of money they need. I don't believe it's necessary to make sacrifices like these to have your dream. That is, it's not necessary to forfeit anything you want, providing you are clear about your dreams.

When you are passionate you are focused, intentional and determined. Your body, mind and heart are all moving toward the same goal in unison. Richard Bach in his book, *The Bridge Across Forever*, tells us that "passionately obsessed by anything we love—sailboats, airplanes, ideas—an avalanche of magic flattens the way ahead, levels rules, reasons, deserts, bears us with it over chasms, fears, doubts."

Passionate thinking is a driving ambition. It comes from a place within you that provides emotional reinforcement. This energy is what you want to harness in propelling your dreams into reality, and I designed the Passion Pyramid to help you do it.

The Passion Pyramid is a tool. It will help you see how to get from where you are to where you want to be, while keeping you balanced in all the areas of your life. It is designed to help you bring more of what matters to you and what you love into your life, at work and at home, everyday. As you strive to make your dreams come true, the information you put into the Pyramid is the foundation on which everything else rests.

You will find a copy of the Pyramid on the preceding page. Use it to align the "four Ps" that can ignite your dreams—purpose, passion, possibilities and power. When used properly, the Pyramid can help you design a blueprint for achieving what you want, and for streamlining the process of reaching your dreams. Like any stable structure, the Pyramid is intended to be read and used from the bottom up.

Most of us live our lives from the top down. Then something happens—a "fire" that needs to be put out, or something to which you must attend. You look at your calendar (scheduling) to see when you can fit it in. Sometimes, if you're lucky, the activity may be related to a project you're working on or one you intend to start. If you're *very* lucky, the venture may even filter down into one of your dreams.

However, when you start working from the top down, whatever you're doing does not come from your Purpose. You want to get to the top eventually, because that's where the rubber meets the road and where things actually get accomplished. To live a life that's filled with passion, you need to start with Purpose and build up from the base. Let's look at how the sections of the Pyramid show up in the world.

Once you have established your Purpose,

you will be able to develop projects

that will take your dreams

out of your imagination

and make them part of your reality.

Purpose: Your Purpose is the foundation; it answers the question, "Who Am I?" Some people think they've known the answer to that question for years. Then, like the captain in the Real People story at the end of this chapter, they are surprised to discover a "different" truth. Later, we'll go through an exercise to answer the question, "Who Am I?"

Dreams: Once you have established your foundation and you know who you are, you can start to look at how you want your life to be. For example, if your Purpose, like George's, is to live life as an adventure, your dreams might include bringing adventure into everything you do, or into a specific aspect of your life like your business or your marriage. All of these are expressions of George's Purpose, "To live life as an adventure." Larry's Purpose, to live life in partnership, helped him to understand his dreams for an extraordinarily close marriage, and for powerful partnerships that generate profit. With clarity of Purpose, your dreams develop a deeper meaning. This is so important.

Projects: Standing in your Purpose, you will be able to develop projects that will take your dreams out of your imagination and make them part of your reality. Not only will your projects be "real," but they will further the journey toward your dream by having built-in, specific, measurable results. Your projects are the means and measurement for accomplishing your dreams and making them real.

Scheduling: Scheduling, at the top of the Pyramid, actually puts your projects onto the calendar, giving you dates by which to meet your objectives and make your dreams come true.

The Passion Pyramid

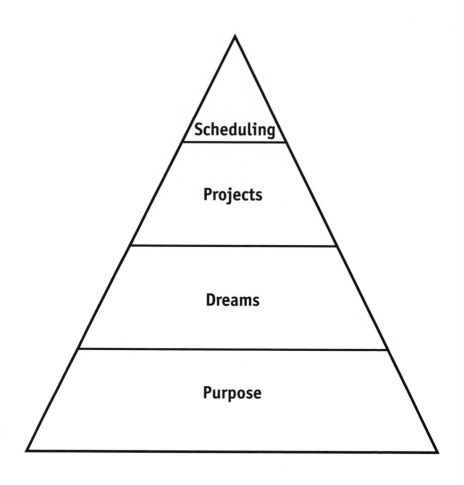

Scheduling

Projects

Dreams

Purpose

The good news is that most of your time is spent doing things you love, not just more busy work.

Having assembled the Pyramid, there are three supporting elements that come into play—possibilities, power, and passion.

Possibilities: Looking at the possibilities in your life from the vantage point of your Purpose, you will feel a new level of power and energy. You will see opportunities where you never saw them before, you will have new perspectives about what you can make happen in your life, and you will allow yourself to remain open to new and opportunities.

Power: The power to live your dreams every day results from your ability to be "in action" on your dreams and to measure the specific results of your projects.

Passion: Standing figuratively and emotionally in your Purpose, you will realize that passion permeates everything else. Your Purpose is what compels you, and kindles the passion to make your dreams come true.

Notice how the sections of the Pyramid interconnect. For example, passion lives in all areas of your life, but it takes on special meaning as you bring it into your dreams; possibilities can be seen from every vantage point on the Pyramid, but they start to show up in ways you can recognize when you move from dreams to projects. The process is not linear; it is holographic and multidimensional.

Marcia's Passion Pyramid

I describe my own Purpose in life as "joyously self-expressing." How do I know?

Passion permeates everything.

Because this is when I am the happiest and feel the most alive.

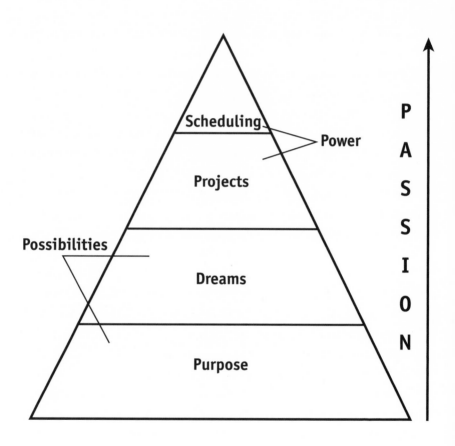

The Passion
Pyramid

One of the highlights of my life was to win my eighth-grade speech contest. I had such fun and creatively spoke about being the first woman astronaut. Once you meet me (which I hope will happen soon), you see instantly that "joyously self-expressing" is who I am. Memories of passionate moments in your life will help you find your purpose, as you will see shortly.

I believe in putting everything I want into my dreams. One dream that symbolizes my Purpose is to travel the world in style and elegance, speaking publicly about something that will make a positive impact on people. I decided to travel on a luxurious cruise ship as a guest speaker, offering workshops about making dreams come true. My project, one of any number I could have created, was a clear expression of my Purpose—to joyously self-express—and an obvious representation of my dream. Because of the passion I felt, I knew that the project was completely consistent with my Purpose.

Once the specific, measurable results of the project were defined, it was easy to get into action. As I gained clarity about what I wanted and created a project to achieve it, the big results easily happened. I spent the Christmas holidays cruising the Hawaiian Islands, all expenses paid for two.

Don't sabotage yourself by trying to deal with the Pyramid from the top down. For example, most people have a negative reaction to "Scheduling," because they feel anxious about finding time to take on additional tasks. Starting at the top of the Pyramid rarely, if ever, allows you to build a life you can live on purpose. Rest assured, however, you will accomplish things faster and easier when you are passionate and on purpose.

When I first started doing this work some years ago, I used to say, "Every day I'm doing something that I love." Now I can say, "I'm *always* doing things that I love." My office is devoid of files, except for project files. Since the projects come from my dreams, which come, in turn, from my Purpose, I am living a life that I love, one that is filled with passion. Whenever I have extra time, which I often do, I reach for one of my project files. I love working on them because I know that doing so puts me constantly in action on the life I intentionally created for myself.

Real Stories: The Captain

The "Captain" had achieved what he thought was his life's dream. From the time he was seven years old he had dreamed of being a ship's captain. He held onto the dream for such a long time that, when he actually achieved it, he wondered, "Is that all there is?"

Passion was missing for him. He wasn't turned on by becoming captain; it was something he'd always thought he would do. After all, his father had been a captain, too.

What had initially been an empowering dream for the Captain had become empty over the years. Now, at age 45, he found himself longing for the next 20 years to pass, so he could retire at 65 and move on to something else. He was appalled; what a terrible waste it would be to wait 20 years to be happy.

Then he started to appreciate that there was a different way to live his life, that he could have a new dream that would allow him to remain a sea captain but bring passion into his life every day. He realized he had a talent for finding solutions to difficult problems, even dilemmas that others thought were impossible to resolve. He began to list his skills and, as he did so, he became aware that he was excited about some of them. He asked me to help him, and we began to turn his passion into projects.

You can live the life that you love

that is filled with passion.

When I last saw the Captain, he was beginning to have conversations with engineering and trading companies, exploring the possibilities for working with them when he wasn't at sea. The best news is that he was excited about potential new opportunities, and enthusiastic about some of the new unpredictability of his life.

Passion is the access to power.

Access your passion

through your Life's Purpose.

He laughed when he told me he had forgotten how much he liked surprises. He had allowed himself to fall into a rut and, until we got him moving toward his dream, he couldn't see how to get out.

Getting in touch with your passion will always get you out of your rut and onto a higher road. We'll discuss further how this can be done in chapter 10, Projects That Move You Forward.

Getting in touch with your passion

will always get you out of your rut

and onto a higher road.

CHAPTER 3

Remembering Your Purpose

The purpose of life is a life of purpose.
— ROBERT BYRNE

IF PASSION IS THE ACCESS TO POWER, the way to access passion is through your Life's Purpose. Your Purpose is who you are, what gets you excited; I might even say that your Purpose is remembering why you're here. We are here to learn, and to grow, and to express ourselves. And we each have great gifts and contributions to make as well.

A client once told me, "I made money and I was successful, but I still felt there must be something else."

"Yes, there's something else," I said. "It's called passion, and it comes from living your life on purpose."

If you're like a lot of readers, you might say, "I picked up this book because I wanted to make my dreams come true, but, between you and me, I don't think I have a Purpose."

Yes, you do. Your Purpose is not a big, burdensome, heavy weight that you "must" accomplish in your life; rather, it's an expression of who you are. Larry, who didn't think finding his Purpose was the way to double his business, didn't increase sales until he defined who he was; then it was easy.

Your Purpose could be anything that gets your juices flowing; it comes from what turns you on in life. The broader you state it the better, because the broader your Purpose the more room there is for passion and possibility. If you're concerned that your Purpose is not going to be "worthy," or big enough, or decent enough, here are some examples that others have offered when asked to complete the sentence, "My life's Purpose is...":

... to live life as an adventure.

... to create joy.

... to help others.

... to make a difference.

... to go beyond.

... to play and have fun (yes, this too is a noble and worthy purpose).

Your Purpose is anything that touches your heart and makes a difference to you. If you're working at a job just for the money, and what you're doing doesn't make you feel proud, perhaps you've lost your sense of Purpose. The test is how you feel: are you turned on, or do you rationalize by saying that if you don't "sell this product, somebody else will?"

Most people are so busy reacting to the needs of daily life that they're happy just to be getting through the day. It's hard to live on purpose when life revolves around daily crises and you're always feeling overwhelmed. By taking the time to define your Purpose, you'll open up more time and space, have more energy, and be more focused. Then your life can change for the better.

Your Purpose is who you are

and what gets you excited.

Your Purpose is remembering why you're here.

Defining Your Purpose

You may be wondering how to determine your Purpose. Don't worry, you don't have to do it all at once, and certainly not permanently and for all time. Life ebbs and flows, and your Purpose may modify accordingly over time.

When I first started speaking about my own Purpose, I didn't describe it as "to joyously self-express." I began by looking at what I enjoyed doing. I decided that I liked to talk and travel, so I defined my Life's Purpose as "Talking and Traveling." Over time, that description was honed and sharpened, and yours will be, too; the more you work with it the more it will start to resonate as a unique definition of who you are and who you are passionate about being.

Recently I watched a rerun of the movie *Fame*. Remember that scene when the keyboard player's father, the cab driver, pulled in front of the school, threw a huge speaker on the roof of his taxi and started blaring his son's music? All the kids came running outside and started dancing wildly in the streets. This made me cry tears of passion, because here was what I love most, joyous self-expression.

Eventually, you will create a way to speak about your passion that really describes it for you. This is important. The five-minute exercise on the next page will help you begin to get in touch with your Life's Purpose by reviewing a few of your special memories. One place to look for what turns you on is to see what has turned you on in the past. Don't think that your life is devoid of these experiences, everyone has them.

Your passionate memories may be include graduating from college, meeting a spouse, getting a big raise. They may include a special trip you took, having a baby or accomplishing an important goal. If you can't find at least three memories of passion—and I promise you've had at least thirty-three, maybe three hundred and thirty-three—you're being too hard on yourself and setting your sights too high. Memorable moments come in all sizes.

It doesn't even matter if you harbor negative reactions about them, since anger and frustration can be mighty motivators. When you look back now, were you excited? Did you feel good? If you answer "Yes" to those questions, write it down.

When the exercise is completed, take a deep breath and relax; the hard part is over. Now look for the pattern, the common component that made you feel good about those memories. What was present for you in all three examples? What were you passionate about?

If you think at first that there's nothing consistent about the listed deeds, bring your mind back to the time and place of each situation. Get in touch with what you were feeling then, about the events and about yourself. Avoid narrowing things down; try to stay with broad, generic statements. Perhaps all the items listed were fun—they all had a partnership component—or they all made you feel uneasy at first, but you did them anyway.

The commonality need not be that all the events happened in the same season of the year; what you're looking for is the consistency of how you felt in each case—who you were being—not what was happening externally. Perhaps the accomplishments all went beyond what you thought was possible, or they led to other things that you hadn't even considered. Maybe there was a quality of surprise connected to them, or they were things you made happen against all odds.

The broader the common thread is the better.

Getting In Touch With Your Life's Purpose

List below three times in your life from the day you were born to this moment when you felt excited and passionate. Look for three special moments about which you can say, "I did that; it felt good." It could be something you did on your own or with others, or something you did for someone else. Perhaps it was having your first child, buying your first house, a speech you gave in high school or college, a project at work. Write them down simply and quickly; as you write the first one, the other two will come.

1. _____

_____

_____

2. _____

_____

_____

3. _____

_____

_____

For example, if you wrote down three sports example, what exactly was the common thread of passion for you? Were you passionate about playing, winning, competing or being part of a team? These are very different responses and will take you in very different directions.

Bill Parker, the zone vice president of the Midwest Zone of Old Navy, hired me to teach his team to become Dream Coaches. Bill's dream was that his team would go to the Super Bowl and win. He had measurable goals for achieving this, including being number one in sales and hiring 600 new employees that year. In a zone that grew from $400 million dollars in sales to a billion dollars in sales in one year, Old Navy is filled with people who know how to dream big. Bill's passion for winning inspired his team, and his dream became their dream, as they acquired the skills and resources for achieving their goals and winning.

The acid test is whether or not the consistent element or elements in your memories of passion were something about which you felt excited; however, don't be concerned if passion seems to elude you at first. Some people feel passion about their Purpose as soon as they define it. Others may not be sure if the stated Purpose is something that truly excites them. You may not experience passion until you're in action on a project; someone else may be turned on by the planning process. If you're having difficulty finding the common thread in all three accomplishments, but you were excited by two of them, you're probably on the right track.

Speaking Your Purpose

Using language that incorporates your newly-defined Purpose into your speech will affirm your passion and move you toward having your dream. I call this, "speaking your Purpose," and below I've listed some examples from people with whom I've worked. In each case the three memories are listed, followed by the first try at identifying their Life's Purpose and then their second attempt to speak it in an empowering way. Note that the initial descriptions of Purpose were altered later.

It doesn't matter whether your Purpose is single-focused or multi-dimensional. Imagine using the zoom lens of a camera to capture your Life's Purpose in the most general way. Then play with the picture until the form, sound, and "feel" of it is right for you. The writing exercise on the facing page will help you find validating and empowering words to access the passion in your Purpose and to remember it always.

So if you have a passion for learning and your purpose statement is "To constantly be learning," the next time you are stuck in rush hour traffic and you say to yourself, "What was my purpose again? Oh yeah, to constantly be learning." Then you can pull out those language tapes or books on tape and feel good that you are doing something that matters to you.

Here's one more analogy. When you know your purpose and can instantly recall it, it's like you are walking around with an electrical chord Look for outlets to plug into, so you can express your passion. Your happiness and satisfaction is back in your hands, where it belongs.

**Your purpose in life is simply
to help the purpose of the Universe.**
— GEORGE BERNARD SHAW

Memories of Passion	Purpose
1. Receiving his Certified Public Accountant's Certificate; 2. Being promoted to manager at work; 3. Buying a dream house while selling his old home without a broker.	To add value to everything he does. -or- To make a difference by being different.
1. Growing her business; 2. Having a special relationship with a great person; 3. Rearing two fabulous children.	To use her creativity to alter other people's lives. -or- To inspire people into action.
1. Making it to the U.S. National Racquetball Team; 2. Becoming racquetball state champion; 3. Striving for a professional career in racquetball.	To have fun while being the best that she can be. -or- To go for the gold.
1. Having twin daughters; 2. Experiences in the wilderness; 3. Winning the Small Business Administration's Outstanding Businesswoman Award.	To experience the adventure of people and life. -or- To live life as an adventure.

Speaking Passionately About Your Purpose

Using the lines below, list all the different ways in which you can complete the following sentence so that, when you think about it and when you speak about it, you feel its underlying passion. Use your three memories of passion to help you.

My Life's Purpose is:

_____

_____

_____

_____

_____

_____

Now rephrase your Purpose to speak it in an empowering way. Make it easy to recall:

_____

_____

_____

_____

_____

_____

The next step is to enter your Purpose in the appropriate section at the base of the Passion Pyramid. You will find the Passion Pyramid repeated throughout the book, so you can fill in additional categories as you make choices that will allow your dreams to become reality. You will also find the Passion Scale, appearing for the first time on the next page, duplicated several times in these pages, so that you can rate your passion as we move through each stage. Rate how you feel about your life's purpose. If you are at "interested" or below, see what's missing from your purpose that would "turn you on" and add it. Then rate your passion again.

Here's what I mean. If all three of your memories of passion were around helping others, and your purpose statement is "To help others," if you have little passion around this now, perhaps you are tired. Adding the word easily, "To easily help others," may prove life changing.

To find your passion we looked at past memories. Now you also have the opportunity to look ahead. What qualities or adjectives might lighten up your life and infuse you with more passion? For many, adding the words joyously or easily, can really make a difference.

If you're wondering how by simply adding a word to your purpose statement it can change you life, consider this. You are about to create dreams that are an expression of your purpose. From here you will design the plan to have what you want. Start with a solid foundation.

The more passion you have at the beginning of the process, the easier it will be to get what you want. Create a purpose statement that will be a solid foundation to build big dreams upon.

The Passion
Pyramid

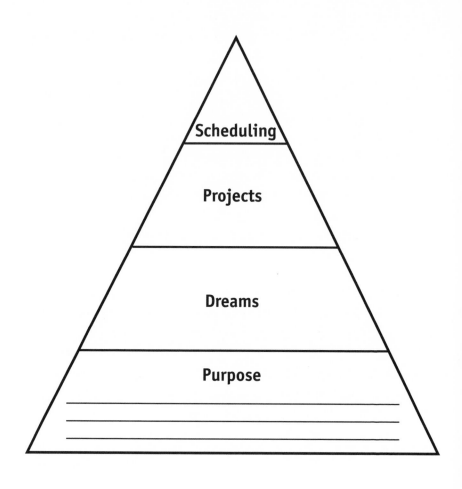

PASSION SCALE

Place an X next to the area that best describes your level of passion about your purpose. Do it right now.

_____ RED HOT*
_____ TURNED ON
_____ EXCITED
_____ VERY INTERESTED
_____ INTERESTED
_____ SOME POSSIBILITY
_____ NO INTEREST

*Note: Some people relate to the adjectives of my passion scale and some don't. Perhaps you prefer to use your own terms, or to use numbers to rate your passion. Whatever works. Just design a simple measurement took so you can continually check in as we move through the process.

Real People: Kathleen

Kathleen was well established as a successful real estate agent, but her real passion was for new experiences and adventure. She told the people who worked with her that her dream of all dreams, now that her children were grown, was to live in Italy.

She got a mixed bag of responses, everything from "you go girl" to "are you out of your mind?" By the time she came to see me, there was no doubt about it. She was moving to Tuscany. With each step she took towards her dream, two things happened. She became more committed and more afraid. By the time she had to put her furniture into storage, she was in need of some real help.

My job was to keep her connected to her passion and her dream. We did this by painting a vivid picture of what her life in Italy would look like. We _made up_ what kind of house she would live in, what her view would be like, what she would do for a living and what she would do for fun. I listened for inconsistencies in what she was saying and how she was saying it. We kept facing and removing the obstacles and really freed her to dream big.

I just got my third Christmas card from Kathleen. She literally is a different person from the woman I met. Year one's card said, "I miss my friends and although I've been offered many jobs, I am keeping my word to you and following my heart." Year two's card said, "I've met tons of friends and have become very involved in the Florentine Community and even started a group to help newcomers. The U.S. Counsel General asked me to serve on the Board of Directors of the Tuscan American Association, to help bring the two cultures together." Year three's card said,

"I've yet to discover my true purpose or destiny but I have learned that timing and patience is everything. I love it here. It has been an incredible life changing experience, that I would do all over again. I feel after taking this big step, I could do anything. I am open to whatever opportunities life has to offer me."

It sounds to be that Kathleen is alive, joyful, having fun and living La Dolce Vita. Expressing your passion and following the dreams of your heart is living on purpose.

CHAPTER 4

Dreams: How Do You Want Your Life to Be?

**Go confidently in the direction of your dreams.
Live the life you have imagined.**
— HENRY DAVID THOREAU

NOW THAT YOU'VE DISCOVERED the passion underlying your Purpose, the focus will be on the direction in which your life will be moving. You'll need some additional tools on the journey to make your dreams come true; in this chapter you'll learn how to formulate dreams that will steer you on the right course.

Perhaps you're wondering about the difference between your Purpose and your dreams. Your Purpose is fundamental: it's who you are. Dreams are mechanisms by which to bring your Purpose, deliberately, into day-to-day life. Dreams answer the question, "How do you want your life to be, in all areas?"

Whether we are in a business environment where we may refer to a dream as a vision or a goal, doesn't matter. What matters is that we have it. I am delighted to see that many companies are using the word dream in everything from advertising to annual reports. An advertisement for Bank of America reads, "The size of your savings shouldn't limit the size of your dreams."

Another for American Express reads, "Who can help you manage the details of your dream?"

The Gap's annual report said, "Where there's a dream, we make it a reality." When I hear this message or one of these companies hires me to talk about passion and vision in the workplace, I feel this is a business that really cares about it's employees and customers.

Dreams also can help eliminate those aspects of life that are inconsistent with your Purpose. For example, my own Purpose is to joyously self-express; some dreams may make me happy, while others may not allow any joy into my life. By measuring my dreams against my Purpose, I can tell if what I've chosen will move me forward with passion to live the life I want, or is it more about a "should," a duty or a self-imposed responsibility. If like me, you tend to be overly goal oriented, this activity is not intended to turn obligations into dreams. Yes, you have to pay the rent and handle other responsibilities, but those activities get scheduled into reality anyway. Creating dreams is about getting your life where you want it to be. For instance, if you have a specific financial issue, create a dream within the economic area that expresses who you are. The financial dream for a person who wants to live life as an adventure may be different than the financial dream for someone who wants to be in a committed family relationship.

Developing dreams is part of the process for gaining insight into what matters or doesn't matter to you. Here we're after eliminating inconsistencies; these dreams are to be fulfilled in support of your Life's Purpose. This is different from the traditional goal-setting process in business, where a desired outcome is selected and a completion date is designated. The funny thing about the goal process is, you set a date to do something and then you either accomplish it, or you move the date.

Dreams answer the question, "How do you want your life to be?"

To achieve your dream, everything from this point forward needs to be done from the perspective of your Purpose. Keep checking in, making sure you're passionate about your dreams. Go for alignment as we move up the Pyramid.

I call this "Living on Purpose." It's essential to "be" the Purpose you defined at the foundation of the Passion Pyramid. Even though you may not feel at ease yet with the stated Purpose, assume that you will; the comfort from living life on purpose will follow. Just trust. Living on purpose is the most joyful and fulfilling way I know to live.

It's too early in the process to expect that everything in your life will automatically align with your Purpose. In fact, while you're learning, it makes more sense to focus on a particular facet of your life. To help you choose which aspects you want to concentrate on, use the Dream Areas exercise on the next page. Decide not only which areas you want to pinpoint, but what there is about them that needs attention.

Perhaps your relationships are boring, and you want to establish relationships that are fun, or find your dream mate. Maybe you want to become involved in your community in a more creative, innovative, or substantive way than before. Use the Dream Areas form to list the facets of your life and what there is to explore about them; there is an exercise later in this chapter to guide you through the actual exploration When the Dream Areas form has been completed, review it and *choose one* category to use as you go through this book. When you've mastered one area by following it through to the book's conclusion, you can go back and use the same techniques to make your dreams come true in the other areas of your life. This process is tried and true on all types of dreams. And if you choose to work on multiple dreams simultaneously, just be sure to follow all the steps for each one completely.

Perhaps you hear a small voice saying

that you can't have what you want,

that you don't have the time or the resources

to take on anything else. Don't worry

about those nagging sounds;

you don't have to "do" anything yet.

Neither do you have to base

new dreams on the past.

Right now, you simply have to

"be" who you say you are;

you can create a whole new life

from this moment forward.

Ask yourself what dreams

a person with your Life's Purpose would want.

Then, listen for the answers.

Remember that your dreams are both the way to incorporate your Purpose into daily life, and a tool for eliminating inconsistencies. Be sure that there is no disparity between the dreams listed on the Dream Areas form and your Life's Purpose. One way to do that is to role play—to "be" your Life's Purpose—and to ask, "If this is who I am as my Life's Purpose, is this an appropriate dream? Does it line up? Does it turn me on?"

Don't carry any dreams over from an "old list" or from what your parents wanted; the values you develop now are the ones by which to live your future life. If you develop dreams that seem contradictory, don't worry that you can't figure out right now how you're going to "have it all."

Suppose you want both a stable home life and exciting world travel. Another way to say this is you want to love your work and still have time to love and be there for your family. You want it all.

My brother works for 3Com and just got back from their European User's Conference, in Monte Carlo. He took his wife, as did the other managers. They wined and dined their customers and had a wonderful time making new friends. Monaco is filled with adventure and romance. Rekindling a little passion in his marriage certainly won't hurt his performance at work. While there, he did have to cut his playtime short one day, to go back to his room for a massage and a conference call. I'm just wondering if he did them both at the same time.

Believe it's possible to take your home life on the road, or that you can have fun at work and that you'll discover a whole new set of possibilities to enable you to have it all. Play with this idea.

You aren't looking for inconsistencies among your dreams, but for dreams that are incompatible with your Purpose. When you respond to the question, "Is this an appropriate dream for my Purpose?" you want to feel excited about the answer. Use the Passion Scale to check in and see how you feel about each dream area.

Eventually, you will want ease to appear in every facet of your life. For the moment, focus on the area you chose to explore throughout this book. The Garden of Possibility exercise found on the facing page, will help you to appraise the dreams in your life, and to align them with your Purpose.

Let's walk through my own example of the Garden of Possibility process that I used to focus on the professional area of my life. I picked this area since one of the things that really mattered to me at the time I did this exercise was re-defining my career. You'll want to choose whatever area is pressing or of interest to you right now.

When I entered the garden, I felt completely at ease, because it was landscaped with my Purpose—to joyously self-express. Seeded with hope, the garden allowed exploration of my professional dream: to have a new career that expresses who I am in the world. Filled with the passion coming from my Purpose, I created the professional dream to have work that's a joyous expression of who I am. That means having work that is play, that is lucrative, and that allows plenty of time for family and friends. Sound like a fantasy? It's not because now that I know what I want, all of it, I can design a plan for getting it.

Should the nagging voice of your doubter begin to surface here, don't fret. We will address your doubts and concerns as we move into the beliefs section. For now, I want to invite you to really begin to dream, to imagine how you want you life to be, without being concerned about whether you believe you can have it or not. That's why I call it dreaming!

Dream Areas to Explore

The categories listed below are aspects of life you might want to explore initially. You don't have to limit yourself to these; select areas that are important to you.

If my Life's Purpose is_____

_____

My Community dream is _____

_____

My Family dream is _____

_____

My Financial dream is _____

_____

My Fitness dream is _____

_____

My Friendship dream is _____

_____

My Fun dream is _____

_____

My Health/Well-Being dream is_____

_____

My Outrageous dream is _____

_____

My Personal dream is_____

_____

My Professional dream is _____

_____

My Recreational dream is _____

_____

My Relationships dream is _____

_____

My Other dreams are _____

_____

PASSION SCALE

Place an X next to the area that best describes your level of passion about your dreams. Do it right now.

_____ RED HOT
_____ TURNED ON
_____ EXCITED
_____ VERY INTERESTED
_____ INTERESTED
_____ SOME POSSIBILITY
_____ NO INTEREST

The Garden of Possibility

This is an exercise to help you create dreams that are consistent with your Life's Purpose. You may want to read this page into a tape recorder, and then play it back. The key to the garden is passion. The passion lives inside your heart and is always present when you're living on purpose. Begin by closing your eyes... take several deep breaths. Relax.

With your eyes closed, envision a beautiful garden in front of you. It's lovely and inviting , and it's filled with your favorite flowers and trees. You easily make your make your way in and feel so at home in this lovely place that holds your Purpose.

Find a comfortable place to sit or lie, perhaps near a shady tree or next to an aromatic flower bed. Relax; you feel completely "at home" living on purpose.

It's a beautiful day; the sky is clear blue with puffy white clouds, and the air is the right temperature. You're completely relaxed and at ease in your Purpose, filled with passion, knowing there's unlimited possibility everywhere.

You reinforce your sense of Purpose by finishing the sentence, "My Life's Purpose is ...." You feel grounded in your Purpose and, from that perspective you begin to look at how you want life to be.

With your eyes closed, look at the area of your life you chose to explore. If you are focusing on the professional area, from the perspective of your Purpose complete the sentence, "My dream in the professional area is to ...." Perhaps you'd like to open your eyes and write it down; if you prefer to keep your eyes closed, fill it in at the end.

After you've finished exploring the area you selected, relax in perfect comfort in the garden. Notice if any images or feelings come up and feel free to write them down as well. Take a last look around and experience the power that envelopes you. Feel the clarity of your Life's Purpose, and know that your dream in the area you examined is in perfect alignment with your Purpose. And that anything is possible.

When you've completed this exercise you will have identified at least one dream in your chosen area. You can have more than one if you wish, but it's less important to designate many dreams than it is to be clear that the dreams express your Life's Purpose.

When you're ready to leave the Garden of Possibilities, breathe deeply. Relax. Open your eyes at your own pace. You will have a clear memory of everything that happened during the exercise. Write it down on the Passion Pyramid: "My Life's Purpose is ...," and, in the area you chose, "My dream is to ...."

In my garden exercise, I focused on my professional life, but that's not the only area for which I have developed dreams. In the personal area, my dream is to develop partnerships with individuals who are creative visionaries so we can produce results that have a positive impact on others. In the area of well-being, it's to be healthier and more physically fit at 45 than I was at 35. In the area of relationships, it's to be in a loving partnership with my life's companion. In the area of friendship, it's to have friends worldwide. In the financial area, it's to shop without looking at price tags. Notice each dream is an expression of my purpose.

Don't be stingy when you develop dreams; put into them everything that you want. When I noted that one of my dreams is to have friends worldwide, I didn't say merely that I wanted friends. I am committed to having friends everywhere on the planet, which suggests travel as another dream. If you don't develop your objectives in a way that expresses your Life's Purpose, your ability to make your dreams come true will be short-circuited.

The power that you experience all around you comes from having passion within you. However, you don't have to be doing this exercise to feel the excitement.

In the designated space on the next page, commit yourself to focusing on a specific area of your life by filling in the blank. Then on the facing page, write your Purpose once again in the foundation of the Passion Pyramid and, this time, include in that box the dream you'll be working on. For example, my own Life's Purpose is to joyously self-express, and my dream in the professional area is to have work that expresses who I am in the world. There is alignment as I move from my purpose to my dreams.

When you fill in the base of the Pyramid, commit your Purpose to paper fully and with passion, and state the dream by which you will live your life on purpose.

Fill in the blank by writing in the aspect of your life on which you intend to concentrate.

I am committed to focusing on a specific area of my life at this time. The area that I'm going to focus on is

_____

_____

The Passion Pyramid

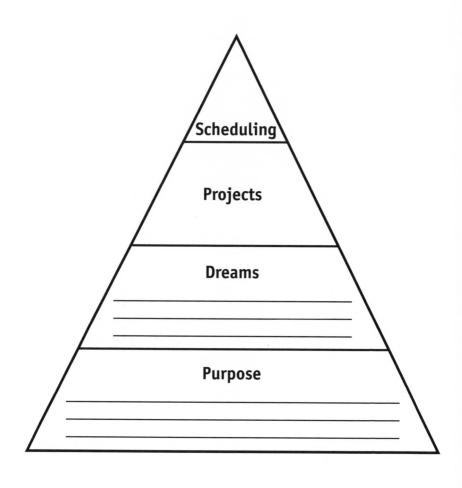

Real People: Beth & Stephen

Since Beth's parents had always worked together, her dream was that she would have a business partner too. She didn't realize it would be her future husband. Beth and Stephen met and married because they loved each other's laugh, among other things. They have a passion for fun. Beth had asked all her previous boyfriends if they would ever leave New York with her and move to San Francisco, which was part of her dream. When she met Stephen and he said yes, she knew he was a "keeper."

They had been married for a year and living in a small apartment when Stephen came home and mentioned that the company he was working for was selling their San Francisco location. The Learning Annex, America's leading alternative adult education organization, offers courses on everything from sushi making to singing, and presents lectures by some of the best selling authors and most highly acclaimed speakers of our time. Beth said, "Why don't we buy it and move out there?" To her total shock, he said, "Okay," and within four months, during one of the biggest blizzards in New York, they packed up and moved west to pursue their dream.

They borrowed money from their family and tapped out credit cards. They had a slow start, since the day they opened their doors, the Gulf War hit. Everyone was home watching CNN and no one was attending classes. Stephen asked Beth to join him, and with her expertise in writing, public relations and graphic design, she got the word out. It paid off. Within one year they also took over Los Angeles, San Diego and eventually, even New York. They are now a thriving business and listed as one of the Top 100 companies in San Francisco.

Beth and Stephen know how to dream. They believed in their dream and demonstrated it. Here are some of Beth's other dreams. Keep in mind her purpose is: To have fun and enjoy life. Her personal dream is to creatively express herself and to empower others to be great. Her professional dream is that their company will be known worldwide for enhancing and impacting the quality of people's lives through powerful, inspirational, nurturing and insightful seminars. Her relationship dream is to have a loving family and be a great mom. Her health dream is to be strong and flexible, physically and emotionally. Her financial dream is to own a beautiful home in a retreat-like setting and her fun dream is to laugh a lot.

As you achieve your dreams, you build confidence and can dream bigger. After years of trying to get pregnant, Beth and Stephen set a date for exploring the adoption process. They heard so many horror stories, but they had learned how to face and break through obstacles. Beth found a potential birth mother on the Internet and when they all met, they loved each other. This mom-to-be had a great sense of humor and felt right to Beth. She was a young, single woman and did not want to keep her baby.

She lived in Missouri where the adoption laws were very prohibitive. If she had the baby there, Beth and Stephen couldn't help with the medical bills and once the baby was born, the baby would have to initially be put into foster care. Beth and Stephen had a different plan.

They moved the birth mother to be near them. Using the Internet again, Beth found her a nice apartment, paid all of her living expenses and doctor bills, and even hired a birth coach. Beth and Stephen were with the mom a lot those last few months, and present at the birth of their beautiful new daughter. Stephen even cut the chord. And Casey Bea, the newest edition to this DreamTeam, laughs all the time. She is a daily reminder that anything is possible when you believe in your dreams.

When you're standing in your Life's Purpose,

the passion is always there and

possibilities live everywhere.

You feel powerful, and capable

of making your dreams come true.

CHAPTER 5

A Dream That Inspires You

All our dreams can come true
if we have the courage to pursue them.
— WALT DISNEY

A DEAR FRIEND ONCE TOLD ME that turning dreams into projects is a way to project yourself into the future. In this chapter, you will learn how to define your dream, how to develop it, and how to initiate it in the form of a project.

Clarifying the dream is the critical component that most people omit, largely because their dream isn't perceived as something real, specific and attainable. If your dream comes from your Purpose, a project can be created to make your dream a reality.

The power to develop a viable project depends, first, on your ability to define your dream in a way that inspires you. The project, which will have specific and measurable results, makes the dream attainable. Moreover, ease will occur as new possibilities open up during the definition phase, and you can start to launch yourself into a different dimension of living life.

Sometimes defining a dream is as simple as choosing a date by which it will happen. Other times, the definition is not as simple as it sounds—having a general idea of how you want your dream to be may not be enough to know exactly how to achieve it.

Clarifying your dream
is crucial for your success.

Describing Your Dream To a "T"

When a dream first enters consciousness, you may not be able to see with clarity what it looks like. Often a dream starts in the subconscious, and remains a nebulous idea floating around in the back of the mind. In order for your dream to come true, it is essential to get it "out of your head."

Speaking of floating, one year at Dream University® Marieta, a woman who had been in the Army for ten years and who now works at the post office, found herself relaxing in the hot tub. There she connected to her passion for being funny. That evening, she came into our workshop and did five minutes of stand up comedy about stamps and life at the post office. Our howling at her jokes gave her the confidence to attend a weekly comedy class, and at 45 years old, she soon wound up at the Punch Line Comedy Club, doing her first showcase. When *More* magazine called me looking for stories about people taking risks at mid-life, I gave them Marieta's name and she wound up with a full page story calling her The Joker.

There are many different ways to gain access to the details of your dream. Some people like to do it through writing exercises; some carry on conversations with others about their dream; and some prefer talking into a tape recorder. One client told me she actually thinks by talking.

Recently I was hired as a spokesperson for a Dream Contest. I traveled around the country appearing on television and inviting people to write a short essay, poem or story about how they would spend money if they won it for the sole purpose of realizing a dream. In this contest called Taste How Good Life Can Be, sponsored by Sunsweet Prunes, we gave away three $50,000 prizes. I like that Sunsweet's criteria was based on creativity and I was surprised at how many entries played it safe and were "realistic" rather than going for their heart's desires.

I hope you will use this opportunity to really dream. I have provided room on the facing page for you to write out all the aspects of your dream. This exercise is a powerful way to get the dream out of your head and allow it to become real. Use the exercise to get in touch with all the resources that can help to develop your dream; use it also to get a clear image of what you want, to get the level of detail behind the initial statement of your dream. Notice whether you believe it's possible to have your dream, but don't let your beliefs limit you. We'll deal with your beliefs shortly.

If you aren't happy with what you write down at first, you aren't committed to leaving it there. Rewrite it, more than once if necessary. As you start to gain clarity, what gets committed to paper will begin to feel right. At the end of this chapter, there are some Real People stories that will illustrate how these techniques work for people who have passion about their Purpose and define their dreams accordingly.

Seeking Inspiration

The specifics of your dream may not all come at one sitting; perhaps it will take a few days, even a few weeks. You may need to seek inspiration to complete the exercise: go to the library, to plays or movies; rent children's videos like <u>Beauty and the Beast</u> and <u>Mary Poppins</u>.

You might want to travel. Keep your eyes, mind and heart open.

Another great place to find out about your waking dream is from the dreams you have while sleeping. No doubt you've heard this recommendation before, but it's worth repeating: place a pad or cassette recorder next to your bed. Tell yourself before you fall asleep to remember your nocturnal dreams, and eventually you will. In fact, you can plant a question in your subconscious before going to sleep –"I want more information about this decision I have to make"—and see what comes up during the night.

You can also daydream by relaxing and letting your mind wander. Be alert to what excites you: perhaps you admire someone's beautiful office, somebody's lovely home, parts of a job someone is performing. When you are building your dream and delineating its details, feel free to include in your dream what you like about other people's reality. This is one place that "plagiarizing" really pays off.

Perhaps you're a woman who wants a beautiful dress from a particular designer. Maybe your dream can start with something small, like an accessory or a great pair of new shoes. Make an investment in yourself and bring part of your dream into reality; you will be that much closer to having it all.

If you dream of traveling around the world, but you don't have the time or money right now, start where you can. Take a day trip, go on a hike, go to a nearby lake, stream or ocean. Don't deprive yourself of something, just because you can't have it all. Every step you take towards your dream puts you closer to your desired result.

The Details of My Dream

Complete the following sentences with as many details of your dream as you can summon. You can put your definition into sentences, you can use a skeleton outline, or you can draw pictures.

Play with it; use your imagination; try different alternatives. Write down something that you want in your dream and, if it doesn't feel right, change it. You are the author of your own dream. I hope you need more space than this to do it.

My dream, or the essence of my dream, is _____

_____

_____

The details of my dream include _____

_____

_____

_____

_____

_____

_____

_____

_____

_____

_____

If there is something simple

that can be brought into your life right now

that will make you feel good,

do it and begin to live your dream immediately.

Some people can focus the images of their dream by using photographs. Perhaps you want to live near the ocean and have a view of the mountains. Find a picture of what you want, put it into your reality by posting it on the bathroom mirror, and start connecting to it. If you begin to think about it as existing now, it will become real.

Whatever you do to stimulate your mind, pay attention and notice what feels good. Relax and have a good time. You are creating a design for your life, letting your dream come forward and elaborating on it. Remember, this is your dream; you don't have to choose what you don't want, or what you think you should have, or what you've always had, or what your mother wanted you to have.

Start by thinking about it as real, by visualizing it and expanding on your visualization. Learn to speak about it clearly; the more you speak about it the more detailed it will become. Write, plan, and brainstorm about it. Get into action, any kind of action. It's your dream; start living it now.

Now, rate yourself on the Passion Scale. How do you feel about the possibility of your dream? Place an X next to the area that best describes your level of passion about your dream. Do it right now.

PASSION SCALE
_____ RED HOT
_____ TURNED ON
_____ EXCITED
_____ VERY INTERESTED
_____ INTERESTED
_____ SOME POSSIBILITY
_____ NO INTEREST

Real People: George
George's Purpose, to live life as an adventure, was embodied by his general desire to bring adventure into every facet of his life. However, George was having trouble finding a way to accomplish his dream, which was to take a lengthy, luxurious, fishing trip to a tropical location.

When George first started to speak about his dream, there were many "reasons" why he couldn't have it. The more he spoke about it the more committed he became. Once he learned to stand in his Purpose, the dream stopped living as a fuzzy thing in the back of his mind and started to take on structure. He began to paint a word picture of what the dream would look like. His described how he was going to get from one location to another, and the detailed components of his dream.

George asked himself questions and gave himself answers, putting into writing exactly what his dream would look like. The first question George asked was how long he wanted the dream trip to be. He was surprised to discover that he wanted it to last at least a month. Who else was with him? He was alone. Where was he living? It was a tropical paradise.

As he wrote, George came up with more and more questions, and as he answered them he became more and more clear about his dream. He put everything into his dream that he wanted and left out everything he didn't want. For instance, he decided to forsake his alarm clock and sleep until he awakened naturally. Even though he was living in a tropical paradise, he still wanted the *Wall Street Journal* delivered daily, because he didn't want to be completely out of touch with the world. He didn't want to do any cooking, so he saw himself jogging on the beach and returning to a delicious breakfast prepared by a chef.

Then George started to ask more about how he spent the day. He visualized owning a small fishing boat; he saw himself using the boat to take fishing trips, both for fun and for the opportunity to meet other people. He kept designing into his dream all that he wanted. George also expressed some concern about being away for an extended period of time. He wondered what impact his trip would have on the people and the business he was leaving behind. He tempered his anxiety by answering these questions positively: he decided, and his family verified, that they would function well in his absence, and that his business would continue to thrive.

Picture yourself
already living your dream.

Once he was clear about his dream, George resolved to try it out on a short-term basis. He determined that, within three months, he would take a two-week fishing trip to an exotic place. He chose Costa Rica, he scheduled it, and he went.

George had a wonderful time, and he learned a few important things. The first lesson was that two weeks was long enough. The fishing was great and so was the adventure, but he missed his family and, after two weeks, he had had enough of doing the same thing every day.

He also observed that bringing adventure into his life deepened his relationship with his family. There's renewed romance in his marriage and, now, anytime he chooses to do so, he's able to bring adventure into many different areas of his life. George discovered, and you will, too, that one magical adventure can lead to many more, if we stop holding back and go for what we want.

Real People: Lynn

Lynn had been working in her position as a vice president of marketing for many years.

She was burnt out and knew exactly what she wanted. Her dream was to have 52 vacation days a year without cutting her salary.

She proposed this to her president, who at first had a hard time swallowing it. But she was skilled at painting a picture and showed him the benefits. She pointed out how she could get the company operating at maximum efficiency and that she would train her staff to function well, without her being there on a day to day basis.

When Lynn took a little more time, she got crystal clear about her true dream. What she really wanted and was passionate about, was travel. This meant she needed freedom and flexibility. Getting an extra day off here and there or going to a four-day workweek was not what she needed.

Lynn shared her dream with her boss and started to prepare the people under her for the transition. When the negotiations were done, she got what she wanted. She went part time, working 80% of the time, without any cut in pay.

Then she realized there was something that she had left on the table. Her company barters with United Airlines, they trade baked goods for airline tickets. If she could get some of those tickets, that would be a dream come true. She went back in and told her boss that there was one more thing that would really make her happy. They agreed she could have eight of the free roundtrip tickets to help fulfill her dream of world travel. Even after she achieved her dream, she kept the door open, and another wonderful opportunity surfaced.

Ask for what you want.

Real People: Brian

Brian's Purpose was to make a contribution to society. His professional dream was to use his skills and expertise in a career that he loved. His project was to start a new business and to own his own company.

The problem was that Brian didn't know what his new company would do. He had a general sense of what he wanted, but he was stymied about the particulars.

Following his passion, Brian decided to create a problem-solving organization for designing and implementing social projects for children and their families. Then he set a specific date, selecting the first of the new year by which to be open for business.

Still, Brian didn't know what his dream looked like. As he flushed out the details, he saw that he could train people to become community leaders. He envisioned creating a variety of products that would further his mission —a children's radio show, a newsletter, periodicals about literacy, a videotape training series.

Now that Brian could "see" his new company's form, he was to define where it would be located, how his office would be decorated, what the logo would look like, who would staff it, how they would be perceived in the community, and where he would get funding. The clarity of his dream kept him inspired and in action. As he moved forward, his next steps became more obvious and, in turn, he became more motivated than ever. There was no stopping him now.

Discovery consists of seeing
what everybody has seen and
thinking what nobody has thought.
— ALBERT SZENT-GYORGI

Real People: Larry

Larry, whose Purpose was to create powerful partnerships and intimate relationships, had as his dream to become a partner with anyone at any time that he chose. At first Larry's dream was to double his business—a big dream without any definition. Envisioning the details of what his dream would look like, Larry imagined that his company would have earnings of $3 million by the end of the year, and $10 million within five years. Keep in mind, he simply made this up and stated it as his dream. This was an essential step.

The more you speak and write

about your dream,

the sooner you'll live it.

The more Larry wrote about his dream, the more specific he became. He wanted everyone in his company to be working in partnership. He wanted to be well known, and respected as a leader in his field. He wanted the people with whom he worked to have the best credentials and to offer the highest quality service.

Larry chose a date by which he wanted to have at least three domestic offices, although eventually he wanted branches worldwide. He wanted to be the owner of his office building and have his name on the outside of it. He wanted a personal assistant, a right-hand person who would take good care of him. His dream was that this person would make his job and life easier, while fulfilling their own dreams.

Finally, Larry understood that it was possible to determine how the whole dream would look, not just the financial aspect that had been his first concern. Gaining clarity about the entire dream, Larry was able to create projects that would help him easily achieve it.

The bridge to make

all dreams come true

is our thoughts and our words.

It all starts here.

CHAPTER 6

Where You Are and Where You Want To Be

**We can chart our future clearly and wisely
only when we know the path which led to the present.**
— ADLAI E. STEVENSON

YOU HAVE BEGUN TO GAIN some clarity about where you want to be in life, but the road to your dreams starts with where you are now. You can't travel that road successfully if you don't know where you are now, or if where you're standing is made of quicksand.

An honest assessment of your current situation may lead to the disappointing discovery that you're not even close to where you intend to go. Sorry, I know reality can sometimes sting, but it is an essential part of the dream formula. Your challenge is to use whatever your existing position is, no matter how far it is from the dream, as a tool to create the momentum to move forward.

I can't stress enough the importance of making an honest assessment of where you are now. Starting with inaccurate information will lead to erroneous decisions about what has to be done, and how far you have to go, to reach your dream. You cannot design your new life on a strong base if you deny any part of your present existence. Get everything out on the table; list where you are with respect to each of the facets. Be brutally honest, but don't become discouraged; everyone has a number of perceived impediments to having the life they want.

Where you are now

is simply where you are now.

There is no value judgment attached to it.

No doubt you will find that you're at a different place within each aspect of your life—closer to your dream in some and farther away from it in others. That's a typical pattern. Ask yourself where you are not only with respect to your dream, but with regard to your support system, your financial aspects, and your feelings. What are your concerns and beliefs? We'll look more closely at attitudes in the next chapter; right now, it's important merely to recognize that you have opinions about where you are compared with where you want to be.

If you need a clue about where to start evaluating, take another look at the completed Dream Areas form in chapter 4. For example, where are you currently with respect to the personal, professional, health, and family aspects of your life? What concerns do you have in these areas? Do you worry that going for your dream will take more time than there is available? Perhaps you don't believe it's possible to make your dream come true. For now, just notice what you are thinking and what you are feeling. We will work with all of it, a step at a time, as we progress through this together.

Tension Can Be Useful
The difference between where you are and where you want to be can create tension. Am I right? The challenge is, can you learn to use this as a creative force? Can you be more committed to where you want to be? Picture the tension in a rubber band as you pull on it, and the release of tension as you relax the pull. Tension will resolve itself naturally in whatever direction there is more focus. Therefore,

all things being equal, something will move in whichever direction it
is pulled harder.

The difference between where you are

and where you want to be

will create healthy tension

that can move you forward.

Thus, if you put "where you want to be" (your dream) at the top of
the rubber band, and place "where you are" (your reality) at the bottom
of the rubber band, the difference between where you are and where
you want to be will create tension. It's like pulling the rubber band in
two opposite directions; the direction in which you pull harder is the
way the rubber band is going to snap. If you tug it intensely toward
where you want to be, it will snap in that direction; if you pull it toward
where you already are, it will snap back.

The bottom line is this. On a day to day basis, are you more committed to your dream or to your reality? The evidence will be clear in
the action you are taking or not taking. Just watch what you are doing
or not doing. It will be very telling.

If you know with clarity where you want to go, focus your attention
on your dream, and use the information about where you are to propel
you forward. If you find that you're far removed from your goal, don't
despair; the tension in the distance from where you are to where you
want to be may launch you even faster in the direction you chose.

You can't be thrust forward, however, unless you stay clear and
honest about your current position. When you start to negotiate with
yourself—"Oh, it's not so bad; I've been here for a couple of years, a

little while longer won't hurt"—you dilute or eliminate the dynamic. It's the tension that moves you forward.

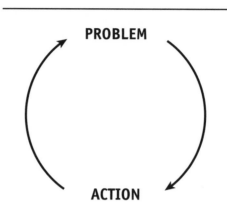

PROBLEM

ACTION

Taking action just to eliminate or minimize the problem will eventually lead you back to the problem.

Problem Solving

There's a different kind of energy involved when moving toward what you want than there is when moving away from what you don't want. For instance, you may have a problem with debt. If you take action to eradicate the debt, you're likely to stop taking action as the problem starts to go away. Your inaction can then lead right back to the problem.

Consider the example of countries whose people are starving. In the past, the action we've taken is to feed those who are hungry. As soon as people are no longer starving, the number of births increase, the population becomes restless, and the problem is increased. In other words, since some progress has been made, people don't try as hard;

they feel they can let up a bit in light of what they've already done, and soon they're back to where they started. Manipulating the problem always leads back to the problem. One solution is to feed those who are hungry while simultaneously teaching them how to produce food for themselves.

To avoid simply manipulating the problem, set up your life so that you're always moving toward what you want. Someone whose dream is to be healthy and physically fit might be 20 pounds overweight. If their dream is to be healthy and vibrant, to feel and look good, a different kind of energy will be applied than to the drudgery of getting rid of the weight by diet and exercise. In the latter scenario, the food intake tends to increase and the exercise tends to stop as soon as the weight begins to drop. When my scale showed I had dropped a few pounds, I would go looking for brownies, until I realized this was a vicious and energy draining cycle. It's this simple. If my dream is to be physically fit and my reality is I am overweight, I can tell which one I am more committed to by what I am putting in my mouth. Once I saw this I began practicing new and healthier habits.

The critical question becomes whether you're more committed to remaining where you are or to getting where you want to be. The difference between the two is what will propel you forward. On the preceding page is an exercise you can use to create a written list of where you are and where you want to be.

Positioning Yourself

List where you are in each of the areas of your life compared to where you want to be with respect to your dream. Be brutally honest; you can't know where you want to go until you know with certainty where you are now. Don't judge; just write it all down.

CATEGORY	WHERE I AM NOW	WHERE I WANT TO BE
Personal	_____	_____
Professional	_____	_____
Family	_____	_____
Friends	_____	_____
Health/ Well-Being	_____	_____
Financial	_____	_____
Fun	_____	_____
Recreation	_____	_____
Relationships	_____	_____
Fitness	_____	_____
Community	_____	_____
Outrageous/Other	_____	_____

As you look at where you are, you are likely to hear an inner voice whispering all your limitations—all your attitudes and beliefs, concerns, fears, worries, and tales about why you can't have what you want.

Fortunately, your positive attitudes and beliefs also will arise—that is, you do believe your dream is possible, it's something you've always wanted, something to which you're committed, something you know you can have.

People frequently sabotage themselves by putting their attitudes, beliefs, or fears into their dream. If you're putting your concerns into your dreams, your fears will become bigger and seem more real as you move closer to getting what you want. Your concerns don't belong in your dream; they're part of where you are now, not where you're going. If your dream is to be successful, keep in the "Where I Am Now" section the fear that you won't have time for friends and family. Assume for the "Where I Want To Be" section that, in achieving the dream, you will have all the time you desire to enjoy your success, your friends and your family.

Creating a record of where you are as compared to where you want to be is an effective exercise. Whether you're writing it out or speaking it into a tape recorder, you will have it available to use as positive reinforcement.

Are you more committed to remaining where you are or to getting where you want to be?

Reread the exercise or play back your recording of it whenever you want to ensure that where you want to be is clearly defined, and devoid of your fears about getting there.

Real People: Tatiana

When I was president of the National Association of Women Business Owners in Washington, D.C., the position afforded me some wonderful opportunities. One of my favorites was, I would often have the pleasure of meeting with woman from all over the world. One afternoon I met Tatiana for tea. She was visiting from Russia.

"I envy you," she began, "because you are a woman business own-er." I was confused,

"Tatiana, you're a woman, you have a business, I don't get it."

"I don't charge for my services." She explained that she was an art dealer, but she didn't believe her artists could afford to pay her. I had an idea.

"Tatiana, I am exploring doing business with your country. Can I ask you some questions?" She was eager to comply.

After about ten minutes, I thanked her and told her that I believe in paying for information. At first she refused, but when she saw I was only talking about one dollar, she laughed and took it.

I said, "You have just been paid for a service you provided. You are now a woman business owner."

A year went by before I saw her again. She pranced in to my office and announced that now she was indeed a woman business owner.

"I went home and started to charge for my service. The amazing thing was they were willing to pay me. I represent some of the finest artist s in my country and one is a goldsmith."

She showed me a beautiful gold charm, a box that she was wearing on a chain around her neck. I could see there was something it. It was the dollar bill that I had given her.

"You believed in me before I did. But once you helped me see what was possible, I knew it was what I wanted."

Real People: Marilee

I met Marilee at a business function/cocktail party. She was ea-ger to share her dream of moving from being a first grade teacher to becoming known worldwide as a great clothing designer. I became exhausted as she mapped out for me what sounded like the longest, hardest road imaginable.

"Do you really think it needs to be that hard?" I asked. She was intrigued and asked, "How would you do it?"

"Do you have talent? Are you good?"

"I am very good," she confidently replied.

"Then bank on your talent. Prove that you are more committed to your dream then you are to your reality or your doubt, by taking action."

A few weeks later a package arrived at my home from Marilee with magnificent sketches of outfits for me. One was a hot pink skirt and pants suit, one was a sexy little purple dress and one was a red evening gown, with a caption under it that said, "I picture you wearing this for dinner at The White House." Although I have yet to be invited, I was relieved to know that I would have something to wear. And I loved that she was dreaming for me. I called her and said, "Make the outfits." Which she did.

Besides being on her DreamTeam by purchasing the outfits, I told some friends, and then the word was out. Marilee told me the greatest gift that I gave her, was when I said," These are fabulous. I believe in your dream." With that vote of confidence, she enrolled in the Fashion Institute of Design Merchandising, and in less than three years and with an investment of $17,000, she graduated with a 4.0 average.

Marilee has been invited to design women's golf wear, band uniforms, and at the Los Angeles County Museum of Art, someone wanted to buy the jacket off her back and produce a line of them. At this point she must reassess, because where she is and where she wants to be, is very different than where she was three years ago.

She sat down and wrote a compelling letter to her dream company, Liz Claiborne sharing her vision of being a top executive designer for them. But then fear and doubt kicked in. As a single mom, with a young son who has diabetes, she has real concerns. As a teacher (which she still is) she has a pension and a good salary. The idea of becoming as associate designer and initially cutting her salary in half, was terrifying. To date, she has yet to mail the letter to Liz Claiborne. She's afraid they'll hire her, and then what?

Marilee is at a critical juncture. Her commitment to her dream was enough to get her to where she is now. The next step is for her to work on her limiting beliefs and to get them out of her dream, before she completely sabotages it. She found a mentor (you'll read more about this in Chapter 12) who told her that her dream job will come if she stays committed to it, believes in it and takes action, one step at a time every day, to keep the dream moving forward. I couldn't have said it better myself.

CHAPTER 7

Breaking Through Barriers and Beliefs

**Your beliefs are never neutral. They either move you forward or
hold you back. And, you choose what you will believe.**
— MARCIA WIEDER

EVERYONE HAS ATTITUDES and beliefs about the aspects of their lives.
Your opinions are long-term parts of who you are: if you're 30 years old
they've been developing for 30 years; if you're 40 they've been evolving for 40 years. Attitudes and beliefs are not always negative and not
always barriers to achieving what you want; even if they are, fear not,
it's possible to use them to your advantage.

The decisions and choices you make ultimately result from the attitudes and beliefs you hold about everything in your life. The process
looks like this:

Your Attitudes & Beliefs
<create>
Your Thoughts & Feelings
<which determine>
Your Choices & Decisions

Attitudes and beliefs are at the core of how you react in the world.
No matter how or why you developed them, it's crucial that you take
responsibility for them, and that you evaluate them honestly. The na-

ked truth about your attitudes and beliefs in this chapter is as important as your honest assessment in the last chapter of "where you are" versus "where you want to be."

In my workshops I often ask, "How many people believe they can make their dreams come true?" A few hands go up. Then I ask, "How many believe it's *possible* to make your dreams come true?" Most hands go up.

"So what will it take to move you from possible to probable?" I ask.

Then I inquire, "Who's living in the home of their dreams, driving the car of their dreams, is in the relationship or job of their dreams?" Sadly, few respond favorably.

If you believe it's possible to make your dreams come true, yet you don't do it, there's a gap between where you are and where you want to be. This gap is comprised of your attitudes and beliefs. The bigger the negative beliefs, the wider the gap.

Some attitudes and beliefs are positive and supportive of the overall dream, and you can use them to get what you want. However, your negative attitudes and beliefs may become obstacles to achieving your dream. For example, you may believe you can't have what you want, or you can only get a portion of it, or that getting what you want will create more problems so it's better not to try. You might think that you're facing barriers you can't move beyond: your gender, your height, your lack of education, and your work experience.

Attitudes and beliefs are never neutral. They either move you forward or hold you back. The most important point I can make here is this. We choose what we believe. Whether you choose a negative or a positive belief, it's much more effective to deal with it now than later.

My Beliefs

Create a list about where you are and where you want to be:

CATEGORY	MY BELIEFS ABOUT WHERE I AM NOW	MY BELIEFS ABOUT WHERE I WANT TO BE
_____	_____	_____
_____	_____	_____
_____	_____	_____
_____	_____	_____
_____	_____	_____
_____	_____	_____
_____	_____	_____
_____	_____	_____
_____	_____	_____
_____	_____	_____

Beliefs that are positive are your allies; they're "on your side" as you design the life you want. Those that are negative can sabotage you, especially if they're perceived as the biggest part of "where you are now," or if they get inserted into your dream. By far, the number one way we sabotage our dreams is by projecting our fears, doubts and concerns into our dreams. Become aware of this major sabotaging pattern and you will change your life for the better.

Unexamined negative attitudes can become bigger than your dream, and turn into insurmountable obstacles after you're already on the road to what you want. If that happens, and you're stopped en route, you're unlikely to reach your dream.

Alternatively, negative attitudes and beliefs don't have to be as menacing as they may seem at first. Re-examine the Positioning Yourself exercise in chapter 6, and note that each of your beliefs is just one of many components within a given area in the "Where I Am Now" column; no single one of your beliefs comprises the whole column. Confront and handle those attitudes now, and they can be used effectively to propel you toward where you want to be.

I am often asked how it's possible to get in touch with your beliefs, when it's widely known that people spend long periods in therapy to explore their deep-seated attitudes. By the time most people reach this stage in the process of making dreams come true, they have little trouble voicing a wide range of attitudes and beliefs, particularly those that hold them back. Here's a roster of the ones I hear most frequently:

I don't have the time, the money, the resources, the skills, and the knowledge;

I'm not successful enough, not good enough;

I'm too successful, too young, too old, or too resistant to change; etc.

I'm in the wrong geographical location;

I don't have any knowledge in that area;

I missed my opportunity years ago;

My energy is too low;

It's too hard, too technical for me;

I don't think I can learn what I need to know;

I don't trust myself or anyone else;

I worry about what others will think;

I don't believe it's possible, so why bother?

In an uneven economy the attitude I hear expressed most often is, "I don't have the finances to handle it." I ask, "How much do you need?" The most common answer is, "I don't know, but I know I don't have enough."

Sometimes not having enough is a reality, but sometimes it's a limiting belief, and usually there are creative alternatives for handling this issue. Frequently however, the very people who express reservations based on their finances are the ones who can't afford to stay where they are. From an economic perspective, they would benefit from making a change.

REAL PEOPLE: CAROLL

When Caroll first heard me speak at a Leadership retreat she said to me, "I want to come to Dream University® but, I can't afford it." She followed up angrily declaring she was sick of hearing herself say those words.

The next thing she said surprised us both, 'I'm coming to DreamU," she said. "I don't know how I will afford it, but it's time for a break through in my life around money." She asked me to be on her a Dream-Team, and I asked her to make it easy for me. "Fine, call me in a week for my credit card number."

I *do* have the time, the money, the resources,
the skills, the knowledge.
I'm successful enough, and good enough.
I'm old enough, young enough, and flexible enough.
I'm in a good geographical location.
I can accomplish this anywhere.
I have the knowledge in this new area.
I have a good opportunity before me now.
My energy is high.
I believe in me.
I can learn what I need to know.
I have no worries about what others will think
I believe it's possible.

She called me the next day. Her husband came home from work, opened the mail and said to her, "This bond we have is a dog. Sell it and pay off your credit card debt." Which she did and she had enough money to pay for her tuition in full, and to cover her airfare to that particular retreat, which was to be held in Maui.

Caroll came to the workshop, and over and over she kept seeing where she said no, where her limiting beliefs were having her play it safe, and where she was killing off any new possibilities. After a week of this, we rewired her internal circuitry.

Upon returning home, everything appeared different, because what had changed was her. Within six months, her business doubled, she received a big promotion and was acknowledged by the president of the company in front of all her peers. In her personal life, she decided she wanted the perfect relationship, and the person she wanted it with was herself. She spent the next year and a half learning more about herself and how to relate to others, cultivating new friends and ultimately decided to end a marriage that no longer supported her vision. She now has a new life of freedom and joy, is good friends with her ex-husband, and is happily dating at age 46.

She recently told me, she has never been happier, she feels totally free, and is facing unlimited horizons, for her career and personal life. There is nothing like releasing the burden of carrying around a boisterous doubter, to free you to find your true power and essence.

The important element is not that you have attitudes and beliefs; it's how you use them. If you think you don't have the resources to get the job done, go back to the previous chapter's Positioning Yourself exercise and enter that belief into the "Where I Am Now" column. If you have a long list of attitudes and beliefs, the whole catalog belongs under the "Where I Am Now" column, whether the beliefs are positive or negative. In fact, interpreting something as a "good attitude" or a "bad attitude" doesn't make it good or bad. It's just an interpretation.

Do your beliefs empower or impede you? One day while working at my health club, I saw Greg. He was a handsome man, about age 38. He was staring off into space.

I jokingly said, "C'mon, aren't you here to work out? Get going!"

He said he was thinking about the year ahead and about some goals he had set.

"Like what?" I asked.

"I plan to be walking by the end of this year," he replied, as he crawled off a Nautilus machine and reached for the wheelchair I hadn't noticed. He explained that he had been in the wrong place at the wrong time, got caught in a crossfire, and was shot in the leg. His doctors thought it was a miracle that he lived through the night, and they told him and his family that he would never walk again.

However, one day, while Greg lay in a hospital bed feeling the futility of his situation, his toe moved. "It just moved," he told me. The doctors assured him it was "nothing," just nerves; but, for Greg, it was the beginning of a new belief. The expectation that he would walk again became the driving force of Greg's life, and he became passionately committed to turning his dream into reality.

I saw Greg recently. Not only was he walking, but he was eager to share his new dream.

"My next step is to find myself a girlfriend and take her dancing. But my five-year goal is to run a marathon. Pretty unbelievable," he chuckled, "for a guy who was told he would never walk again."

Whose beliefs are you buying? What's stopping you from going for your dreams? Anything and everything you want is no more than a belief away.

Interpretations

When something happens in any kind of situation, the results can be interpreted negatively or positively. Interpretation depends on attitudes and beliefs.

If a member of your staff suddenly seems to be doing ineffective work, it could be interpreted as the employee's lack of interest and general unhappiness. On the other hand, maybe the employee is dealing with a problem at home, or is concerned about job stability. Which interpretation is correct? In this case, inaccurate interpretations can be avoided by communication.

Ask the employee what's going on; create a dialogue so you don't have to guess about someone else's behavior.

You can learn to use interpretations to empower you by getting accurate information, and by thinking of outcomes in positive terms. If you believe there are opportunities in everything that happens, the possibilities will appear everywhere. If you take the attitude that you'll "believe it when you see it," chances are you'll never see it. This is an important point; don't glide over it!

Here's how your beliefs can empower or impede you in moving toward your dream. If your beliefs are obstacles, they will trip you up or keep you from stepping out into your dream.

However, if you use your beliefs as tools to help you achieve your dreams, you transform them into stepping stones. Now your beliefs have become the bridge that allows you to move easily from where you are to where you want to be. You decide. Will you use your beliefs as barriers or stepping-stones? How you see and use them is up to you. If you believe in yourself and your dreams, you'll be training yourself to use the power of interpretation to get what you want.

Interpreting an attitude as

"good" or "bad"

doesn't make it good or bad;

it's just an interpretation.

Facing Fear

Imagine that there's a gift in your life, one that's so obvious that every time it shows up it's a direct sign that you're on the right path to getting what you want. Fear can be this gift, and this is how it works.

Everyone's life is about change. Sometimes *you* change, and sometimes something can change your life. Often when you think you have everything figured out, happens, and the course you were on is somehow forever altered.

As a sign on a tip jar in my local coffee shop said, "If you fear change, leave it here." Don't we wish it could be that easy? The truth seems to be that some people fear change, some people resist change, and some people claim to thrive on it. Human beings seem devoted to consistency as a way of life. Yet the only constant is change. What you fear may not revolve around what is being changed; what you call "fear" and associate with a negative belief may be your body's resistance to the act of changing.

You can learn whether you're on the right path to where you want to be by facing fear and acknowledging it as a landmark for change. That's the gift. If you were not moving away from your current identity, if you were not seeking to change your life, you would not be experiencing fear.

Because we think of "change" as filled with murky unknowns, the ultimate fear may feel like death. However, the experience is actually the old you dying away, and allowing you to be transformed. This is good news. By trusting what you want, often you will be able to release the part of you that was afraid of making your dream come true. By shedding the pieces that no longer fit, you can create a new dream to move toward. Fear is actually a measurement tool; it means that you're leaving the old behind; it's a gift that indicates you are closer to your dream.

> **What would you attempt
> to do if you knew
> you could not fail?**
> — DR. ROBERT SCHULLER

Empowering Yourself Out of Fear

Fear can be seen as a healthy and natural mechanism, a sign of vitality, and evidence that you are in process. Sadly, unless you learn to use fear as empowerment, it can also stop your progress dead in its tracks.

First you need to distinguish fear that protects from fear that restricts. When fear keeps you out of dark alleys at two o'clock in the morning, listen to your inner voice. On the other hand, fear of change, fear of moving closer to a dream, or fear of something that you've always wanted is negative and limiting.

Suppose you always wanted a little country home. You've dreamed about the rooms, the yard, the picket fence. One day you find your dream home and you think, "Oh lord, now what?" The thoughts that fly through your mind create fear, and you invent stories to justify why you're afraid.

"I just can't give up my friends and move away."

"I'll never sell my house."

"It's too small or too large for me."

"The commute will be too far."

"No one will visit me out there."

"It was only a dream anyway."

If you see opportunities

in everything that happens,

possibilities appear everywhere.

Take a fresh look at the dream. Start by closing your eyes and reconnecting with the dream house. Assume there are no limiting circumstances like the ones listed above, and ask, "Is this the house of my dreams?" If the answer is "No," you can let it go. If the answer is "Yes," then you can go for it.

It's actually possible to use fear as a way of getting something that you want. Catch up with Ilene, whose story began in chapter 1, to learn how she used fear to launch her dream of running her own dance company.

You may think that Ilene's experience is too neat an ending to her story, but that's just a limiting belief. Maybe you know about someone who's afraid and is unable to devise a powerful or simple solution. Part of having a belief includes wanting the situation to turn out in a certain way; and, often, fear is used to justify the outcome.

Whether or not the situation will conclude as you believe it will, what matters is the meaning you give to the outcome. Will a negative result mean that you're a failure and that you shouldn't go for your dream, or will you be able to accept the outcome, whatever it is? I hope you won't be someone who uses the demise of a dream to stop dreaming all together. Accepting the consequences, good or bad, will free you; take a risk, but be aware that things sometimes turn out differently than you expected. In Ilene's case, facing her fear enabled her to deal with it. If her plan had not worked out, she would have developed another; confronting her fear was empowering.

This Space
Available For
Your Dreams

Thoughts and Feelings

Earlier I mentioned that attitudes and beliefs lead to thoughts and feelings, which in turn lead to decisions and choices. If you want to become aware of your attitudes and beliefs, pay attention to what you're thinking and feeling. Remember:

Your Attitudes & Beliefs
<create>
Your Thoughts & Feelings
<which determine>
Your Choices & Decisions

If your dream is to establish a new career, but your belief is that it's not possible, what do you think and feel about that? Do you feel futility, and resigned to the idea that you can't have your dream? Or, do you think you can have what you want because you deserve it?

Suppose your dream is to be famous. Specifically, you want the *New York Times* to write a front-page story about you, but you don't believe it's possible. The logical sequence of your thought process might be that you don't think it can happen so you decide not to even pursue it.

Keep speaking your dream,

keep speaking the possibility.

Now you have the same dream with a different belief. You believe it's possible to make your dream come true. Your thought process is, "I think I can make this happen," and "I think I know who can help me." Your new choice is to go for it.

Simply changing your belief has shifted your internal conversation from thinking of your dream as impossible to seeing its possibilities. This is an example of removing the obstacles in order to let the opportunities occur.

Real People: Ilene

Ilene, who wanted to become the full-time executive director of her own dance company, feared severing her ties with the people at her current place of employment. She'd been working there for a long time and had developed relationships that mattered to her. She believed that, if she left, the relationships would be over. That belief was somehow turned into a fear that she was going to be alone in her new venture.

When Ilene clarified where she wanted to be, she decided to take her relationships with her. She also realized that one of her skills, writing grant proposals in the field of the arts, was something she could sell to the company for which she'd been working.

Ilene approached her employer and suggested that his company become Ilene's client; her employer, seeing the value in hiring someone on a project-by-project basis, accepted Ilene's proposal. Because she assumed a new role, that of freelancer, the project was awarded to Ilene on her own terms. She negotiated more money, better hours and greater flexibility than she'd had as the company's employee. Without announcing her fears, Ilene was able to use them as a mechanism for getting her employer to "go with her." The important aspect of this is that Ilene identified her fears to herself, and developed a way to deal with them that catapulted her dream into reality.

Simply changing your belief
can shift your internal conversation from
thinking of your dream as impossible
to seeing its possibilities.

Ilene also saw that she had been using her fear for a long time to stop herself from moving forward. There was a gap between where she was and where she wanted to be and that gap was created by her beliefs. When she examined her attitudes honestly, she was able to use them to break through and move toward what she wanted. In fact, she wound up with more than she thought she could have: she didn't just walk away from her employer feeling okay about it; she walked away with a new client, and a powerful relationship with her former boss.

You will find it easier to become aware of your thoughts and feelings now that you're clear about your attitudes and beliefs. It's even possible, once you understand that you have a core belief, to go back and change it. If you alter your beliefs, your thoughts and feelings will change, too. Your changed thoughts and feelings, in turn, will motivate you to examine your decisions and choices. What are the decisions you're making in your life? Are they positive choices that will move you toward your dream, or are your decisions moving you away from things you don't want?

This point is so important, I want to illustrate it again. We often think we know who will or won't help us, or whom we believe will give us flack on our dreams, and then we may be surprised.

When you identify your fears
and learn to use them positively,
you can develop ways to deal with them
that will catapult your dream into reality.

Real People: Renee

Renee was the marketing director for one of the premier motorcycle events in the world, but her dream was to publish a quarterly magazine covering the top motorcycle rallies in the United States.

Renee shared her dream with the sales manager of the Sturgis Rally News magazine, and concerned about jeopardizing her current position, asked that it be kept confidential. Lucky for Renee, her request was not honored, but rather her dream was told to the owner of the magazine. Little did they know, that the owner's dream was to diversify his printing company and enter into magazine publishing.

Renee was hired to launch the magazine and since her dream included not moving because of her son, she is managing this new publication from her hometown (200 miles from the company's main location). They just formed the Motorcycle Events Association, which her new boss financed. This was a dream come true, and by sharing her dream, it became even bigger and more wonderful than she imagined.

Perhaps your dream is to move from the East Coast to the West Coast, or from California to New York, but you fear that such a move would be too far away from your family. That feeling may refer back to an attitude or belief that your family won't love you if they don't see you. Is this belief real? This is a good question to ask yourself about all your beliefs, because the truth is that beliefs are not real. They are something we have created; and we have the power to recreate them at any time.

You can change your attitude by adopting the belief that you can have it all friends all over the world. The new outlook will help you understand that, wherever you're living, family and friends will come to visit you, or you can visit them, and that you'll make new friends easily. Thus, you have adopted a positive feeling about yourself and your place in the world; then, if you decide that California is it, making the choice will be easy.

Some people think it's difficult to change a belief and some people think it's easy; that's just your *belief about your beliefs*. If you have a belief that is getting in your way and is crying out to be changed, The Big Book of Your Beliefs exercise on the facing page can help you do it.

Your attitudes and beliefs can work to empower you or to frustrate you. By confronting doubt and fear, you will allow opportunity to show up. But the door is closed where doubt reigns. You need to believe—in yourself and in your dreams. Then you can make decisions and choices that support making your dreams come true.

The Big Book of Your Beliefs

Place yourself in a quiet spot and relax. Take several deep breaths and prepare yourself for a journey into your mind. Imagine that you're in the attic of your mind. It's filled with lots of dusty memories: your bicycle from when you were three, your mother's wedding dress, old albums.

As you walk through the attic you come to a corner. In the corner there's a beautiful pedestal on top of which is a big book. On the cover of the book it says, My Beliefs. Blow a little dust off of the book, open it and turn to a page where you have a belief that you want to change.

See your belief on that page. You can write in the space below or just picture it in your mind. Whatever that old belief is, read it, and prepare to change it.

My limiting belief that is stopping me from having my dream come true is:

_____

_____

Perhaps you believe it's not possible to have what you want. Read that belief from the page in the book, take a big, black marker and draw a huge "X" through it. Then tear the page out of the book and burn it. Get rid of that belief: cross it out and tear it out. Feel the emotion of finally letting this old belief go.

Now you're left with a clean page in the book, because there was nothing behind the page you tore out. Pick up a new magic marker in your favorite color and write your new belief. Your new belief will correspond to the one you destroyed, but it will be stated positively and in the first person: "It is possible for me to have what I want." Consider adding the word "easily."

Write your new belief expressively and with flair, so that you feel it, and you can internalize it. After you've written it, read your new belief out loud to yourself. Then close the book, leave the attic, and know that your new, positive attitude now lives in The Big Book of Your Beliefs.

My wonderful new belief is:

_____

_____

Do you believe you changed your belief? Do you believe at least that it's possible you changed it? Or do you believe it can't be that easy? What if it is that easy? It's all up to you. You decide whether to believe or not. That's how beliefs work.

CHAPTER 8

The "C" Word—
Commitment

Never, never, never, never give up.
— SIR WINSTON CHURCHILL

NOW THAT YOU HAVE DETERMINED where you are and where you want to be, you'll have to make a choice. Do you feel a greater commitment to having more of the same, or to having your dream come true?

Many of the people I coach find that, once they get to the commitment stage, dramatic things happen. The continuation of some of the Real People stories, found at the end of this chapter, illustrate not only how people move into the commitment stage, but how it happens once the commitment is made.

A priority question to ask is what kind of commitment you're willing to make to achieve your dream. The answer may surprise you, just as the Carters were surprised that they wanted to close the business to which they thought they were devoted. However, once you are committed to making your dream come true, everything seems to move faster, and you seem to know with greater certainty how you need to proceed. Your next step becomes evident, as does the step after that.

I sometimes refer to "commitment" as the "C" word, because a lot of people think of it as if it were an obscenity. Perhaps they view commitment as "locking them in" or "getting stuck."

Until one is committed, there is hesitancy,
the chance to draw back, always ineffectiveness,
concerning all acts of initiative (and
creation). There is one elementary truth the
ignorance of which kills countless ideas and
splendid plans: that the moment one definitely
commits oneself, then providence moves too. All
sorts of things occur to help one that would never
otherwise have occurred. A whole stream of events
issues from the decision, raising in one's favor all
manner of unforeseen incidents and meetings and
material assistance which no one could have dreamed
would have come their way. Whatever you can do or
dream you can, begin it. Boldness has *genius,*
power and *magic* in it. Begin it now.

— JOHANN WOLFGANG VON GOETHE

When I speak of commitment, I mean a covenant with yourself and for yourself; committing to something that you want, to having your dream come true, to moving forward. Commitment is hardly a dirty word; on the contrary, it's a powerful experience.

Nevertheless there are some common attitudes and beliefs that stop people from making a commitment to themselves:

"It's going to force my hand."

"I'll be stuck with it and won't be able to change direction later."

"It might be the wrong move and, if I keep my options open, something better will show up."

"I might look silly.

"It will take longer for me to get there than I care to invest."

"I might not be able to do what I say."

"I might not be able to follow through."

"What if I fail?"

You can deal with "commitment" in a similar manner to the way in which you treated "fear" in chapter 7: you can redefine commitment as something positive, a tool that can be used to propel you toward having your dream, which it is Maybe what you've always needed to reach your dream was to have two thousand dollars; commit to accumulating that sum by a certain date so you can put yourself into action. Commitment is a much more powerful way of living than waiting around and hoping, or worse, never doing anything to make your dreams happen.

"It's going to open up new possibilities."

"I choose it. Life is full of choices."

"It might be a good move, and by staying committed other good things will show up."

"It won't take long for me to get there."

"I may do exactly what I say."

"I will be able to follow through."

"I intend to succeed."

Walk Your Talk

A critical element of commitment is doing what you say you're going to do, actually being as good as your word. It's "walking your talk."

Right now, your dream doesn't exist in reality. It begins to take on life as you envision it and speak about it. During the commitment stage, as you open yourself up to new possibilities, many things can start to happen. If you're not responsible about your commitment, the process will start to unravel and you will undermine yourself and your dream. Get into the practice of following through on your commitment: walk your talk. Maintain integrity.

When you commit, a new dynamic will start to show up, bringing opportunities you didn't know were possible. Be especially careful at this point to avoid being stopped by limiting beliefs and attitudes; sometimes in the commitment phase, self-sabotage can "sneak up" on you when you're least expecting it.

I was so excited about taking my dream holiday in Greece. I had my ticket, a place to stay and I was committed. So why when a client called me with a big job, right smack in the middle of it, did I accept the job, which would mean cutting my vacation time in half? That evening I noticed I was grumpy to the people I love, and became suspicious that something was going on, something that I was not aware of. Then it hit me like a ton of bricks. I was selling out on my own dream. Integrity means keeping your agreements with yourself too, perhaps especially with yourself. The next day I called back my client and apologized, telling her I would not be able to speak at her event. "Why?" she had to ask. I took a deep breath, and for a moment, was concerned about what she would think of me. "I'm going to Greece to pursue a long overdue dream. I'm sorry."

"Why would you be sorry? I'm just sorry I'm not going with you. We'll try to schedule you to speak at our conference next year," she said.

These sabotaging patterns can be subtle and sneak up on you. For example, you might be committed to doing something even though you're worried about not having the time or money to do it. Don't stop acting because of your concern. By acting on your commitment, you open up opportunities—perhaps some new resource that will make the whole thing feasible. You might say that, if you are willing to make the commitment down to the marrow in your bones, amazing things will happen in your life, including the fact that wonderful people will emerge to help you. This is not about being flaky or irresponsible. Show up fully for what you want, even if it takes you into foreign territory.

The Sliding Glass Door Exercise on the facing page will help you learn to live in your commitment. When the exercise has been completed, you may decide not to commit and step through the door. That's fine. Be clear that this side of the glass door is where you choose to be right now. Your dream will always be there on the other side of the Sliding Glass Door. When you are ready, reach out, open the door, and step through.

Real People: The Carters

The Carters, the couple who owned their own store, were committed to having a successful business. They were surprised to learn that their retail operation, to which they had been devoted, was not the kind of success they wanted.

When they understood that where they were wasn't even close to where they wanted to be, the Carters realized that they had to make a decision: did they want more of the same, or were they ready to make a commitment to having their dream? When they decided to live on purpose and move forward with their dream, they did it in a big way. They closed their store and transformed their whole business, to say nothing of their lives, into something else.

Because amazing things happen when we commit, changes started for the Carters. When they recognized how central their relationship was to each of them, they committed to creating a shared goal out of their individual Purposes. Thus, an unexpected outcome was that they became more committed to each other.

The Carters' commitment got them into immediate action. Within three months they had phased out of their retail operation, and created a new consulting business that gave them greater flexibility and the opportunity to be in closer partnership with each other. Their commitment catapulted them into an even bigger, and much better dream.

The Sliding Glass Door

Remove yourself from outside distractions by putting yourself someplace where you won't be disturbed. Relax. Take a few deep breaths. This exercise is completely about you, about stepping into your commitment.

Imagine that you're standing with your nose pressed against a glass door, so close to it that your breath is steaming up the glass. As you wipe away the steam, you see a beautiful place on the other side of the glass. Rainbows, waterfalls, beautiful animals, heaven on earth.

Feel your feet standing on the floor on your side of the glass door, the other side of your dream world. You're standing in the "Where I Am Now," where you live with everything that's happening in your life, including your attitudes and beliefs. Looking through the glass door, you can see the beauty on the other side. You will have the opportunity to find out if the other side is a place that you want to be.

Grasp the handle and slide the door open. A gentle, warm breeze comes wafting in, and there's a delicious smell in the air. You feel warm and welcomed.

As you gaze around, you see everything on the other side that you want, everything that's in your dream, everything you're committed to having. Your family is there, too, your friends, your dream house, your dream life. All the elements of your dream are there, on the other side of the door.

Notice where you are and where you want to be. All you need to do to get to the other side is make the commitment and step through.

Ask yourself, "Is this what I want? Will I commit to this?" If the answer is "Yes," lift your foot and step through.

Now you're on the other side, living in a land of possibilities. Here's where all your dreams can come true. Don't worry if you don't have it all figured out. Just trust: now that you're standing in your commitment, you're standing in your dream.

Take a couple of deep breaths and relax. Once you do, rate your Passion Level. It will probably be quite high. Good work!

PASSION SCALE

Place an X next to the area that best describes your level of passion about your commitment. Do it right now.

_____ RED HOT
_____ TURNED ON
_____ EXCITED
_____ VERY INTERESTED
_____ INTERESTED
_____ SOME POSSIBILITY
_____ NO INTEREST

Real People: Nancy

Nancy, the woman starting a new business at the same time she was pregnant with her first baby, was committed to having balance in her life. For Nancy, that meant having quality time for her husband and baby, and also for her new business.

The issue wasn't about only balancing time; it also was about balancing energy so she would have enough to give to both areas of her life. Nancy's commitment was to be the best that she could be personally and professionally, without selling out on herself.

Everybody has only 24 hours in each day, and Nancy began to think about how she was going to use her allotted time to achieve her dream. Once she understood her commitment clearly, the steps she needed to take became obvious.

Nancy decided that she was only going to work a certain number of days during the week. She built a lot of flexibility into that decision by allowing herself to choose weekly which days that would be. She did not see her overall commitment to her business as amorphous, but she allowed herself to be accommodating in the way she made it work.

She also knew she would need some help to achieve the flexibility she wanted, and she immediately hired a live-in housekeeper. That relieved her both of the concern about child care while she was at the office, and of the need to perform household chores. Thus, when Nancy came home from her new business, she had the time and energy to be with her family. Her commitment to her dreams enabled her to create a balanced life, one that she chose deliberately and loved living.

If affording this kind of luxury seems out of your budget, it can sometimes be done as a barter arrangement with students seeking housing. Commitment comes in many different forms. Get creative. It's up to you.

Commitment leads to action

And action brings your dream closer.

CHAPTER 9

Yes, It's Possible— A Rallying Cry

**You see things and say, "why?" But I dream things
that never were and I say, "why not?"**
— GEORGE BERNARD SHAW

WE BEGAN THIS BOOK speaking about "possibility" as something you can have. In this chapter, you get to play with your dream as if you truly believe it's possible to have what you're committed to, to have all the goals in your life align, to have a life you love, to have the time to enjoy it, and to start right now. Check in with yourself. Does this sound enticing or frightening?

I am talking about being open to a world of possibilities. Having possibility in your life requires that you practice at every opportunity to speak the words, "It is possible," and to believe them. Unfortunately, most of us have been trained to believe that the things we want are not possible. To change that takes retraining. You can learn to hear yourself, and you can educate those around you to hear the possibility in what you say, instead of, "Have you gone mad?"

The assumption that "it is possible" is at the core of having your dream come true. If you have read this far in the book and you confess that you don't believe you can have your dream, confront and handle your negative beliefs before you go on. You may wish to go back and read some of the earlier chapters to identify what's holding you back and how it can be changed. You can't make your dream come true if you don't believe it's possible.

> **What today is impossible to do,**
> **but if it could be done,**
> **would fundamentally change what I do?**
> **— JOEL BARKER**

The Sliding Glass Door Exercise, found in chapter 8, is one of the methods you can employ here. On this side of the door is your belief that it's not possible, but the other side is filled with possibilities. Notice where you're standing: are you on this side, in "I don't believe it's possible," or are you on the other side, standing in your commitment? Choose one.

You can even suspend your negative attitude and say, "I'll believe it for awhile and give it a shot." However, I recommend that you walk through that door. Be committed to having your dream come true, be willing to have it be possible, allow your attitudes and beliefs to support you, and stop holding onto some outdated negative opinion. Step through; that's where the surprises will happen. Being open to possibility means you are open to hope, and hope invites us to say yes to life. From here there are many opportunities to handle all of your concerns and to help move you to the next step.

Moving Into Your Projects

Possibility begins to seem likely when you move forward from dreams to projects. As you start to involve yourself in the specific results, the dream will become animated and take on credibility. If you don't know how to accomplish that, relax; we'll explore how to make it happen.

When you've made your commitment, you will have a different perspective on your dream than you did when you were wondering if it would ever happen. Maybe you once thought you didn't have the time to go after that new piece of business that you want; now that you're committed to doing it, and you've dealt with all your negative attitudes and beliefs, you may see the logic of freeing time by giving up something that doesn't interest you anymore. Your new outlook, that it makes sense to give up something that no longer has value to you, is a direct result of your ability to see where you are, compared to where you want to be. If there is something you don't have to do, and you don't want to do it, why are you doing it? The most common answer surely is, "Guilt." By creating dreams that include the people you love and care about, you can avoid negative and destructive feelings.

Your dream is possible.

Refocusing on your Life's Purpose (who you are and what turns you on) will assist you in deciding when to give up or walk away from something. You'll notice a lighter, freer feeling as you let go of the old and create room to embrace the new.

Living up to your commitments also allows for new relationships, and connecting resources in a creative way that you hadn't considered before. You don't yet have to focus on the specific strategies and steps; look at what else you might put into your dream to have everything you want. Your commitment may even lead you to include items you didn't know about earlier.

For example, in defining your dream now, you might say, "I want an understanding, lucrative, supportive partner." Or, "I will find a venture capital firm that's interested in funding my project." Perhaps you're ready to brainstorm with other people; now that you see your dream clearly and you're committed to having it, you can gather a group of individuals whom you respect, and who can help you decide on the specifics.

Maybe you previously determined that you wanted to live in a particular location, and now you want to put some flesh on that barebones dream: a particular kind of house, a pool or jacuzzi, walk-in closets in which you can see your designer wardrobe. Have fun with this while you allow your dream to grow.

New possibilities also appear when you want to create balance in your life. You begin to see, as Nancy did, that you can be successful in business and still have time to be with your family; that, once you set aside your negative attitudes and beliefs, you can allow yourself to have somebody else cook dinner or help make your life easier in some other way.

The smartest thing I think I have ever done was to hire a personal chef. I contacted the Association of Personal Chefs and found Jeff Parrot. Every two weeks he comes to my home, bringing with him pots and pans, food and spices, storage containers and labels. He spends five hours in my kitchen cooking up a storm. The smells are so wonderful I usually come begging for a snack, which he always graciously prepares. Although I am welcome to hang out with him and get some culinary lessons, I am much more interested in the end product. He hands me my menu for the upcoming weeks and my freezer is filled with healthy, gourmet entrees, side dishes, soups and snacks. I am in heaven. All week long, I eat well, I can have people over and impress them (although I always give credit where credit is due), and I have no pans to wash. These meals wind up being cheaper and much less fattening than eating out every night. I highly recommend it.

The important question, now and always, is, "What else is possible?" At the end of this chapter you will find the continuing story of the Carters, who found many possibilities once they began to live in their commitment. Nancy, the expectant mother with the new business, discovered such possibilities as working fewer days and having live-in help. For Ilene, the woman who started the dance company, the possibilities were to write grant proposals as a freelancer, to provide other kinds of consulting services, and to raise sponsorship dollars for her new venture.

What Else Is Possible?

DO NOT SKIP THIS PAGE; DO NOT SKIP THIS EXERCISE.
When you think you've listed everything that's possible, and you're sure there's nothing left, ask yourself once again, "What else is possible?" I assure you more will come.

What else is possible? _____

_____

_____

What else is possible? _____

_____

_____

What else is possible? _____

_____

_____

What else is possible? _____

_____

_____

On the previous page you will find an exercise that will help you ask yourself, "What else is possible?" Do not skip "What else is possible?" It will help to ensure that you have included in your dream all the pieces you truly want.

Another exercise to help you see what else is possible is called the Looking Back Exercise. Project yourself out in your mind's eye one year from today. Looking back from that point, write out how the last year "was" for you. Remember who you are now: someone standing in your Life's Purpose, whose dreams are deliberately chosen, who has a clear sense of where you are and where you want to be, and who has removed all the limiting beliefs and obstacles.

Through the Looking Back Exercise you can develop a game plan by projecting yourself into the future to look back at the past. You can also understand the feelings and sensations of those events that are *about* to unfold in your life. Because you have become so focused and directed, the high probability is that, over the next year, you will live out your projection. Your dreams will come true.

Be specific when you're "looking back." State your "accomplishments" during the last year. Draw the complete picture for yourself, leaving out none of the details. Remember, you stepped through the Sliding Door.

What were you passionate about?

Where did your achievements take place?

Who else was involved?

What funds became available?

How did you spend the extra money that came your way?

How did others respond?

How did you feel as you passed certain milestones?

How did going down one path take you to another?

Whom did you meet this year that you always wanted to meet?

How did you spend your exotic vacation?

How did you look and feel?

How was that last year for you, now that you made your dream come true?

Looking Back on *This* Year

How this year was for me (if everything was possible):

_____

_____

_____

_____

_____

_____

_____

_____

_____

_____

_____

_____

_____

_____

Let more and more come to you as you're writing; you'll be surprised at how much detail you will have about the "past" year. Make it up exactly as you want it to be. Do not compromise here.

Everything up to this point—all the exercises, visualizations, writings—has been a projection of what you want to have. Now we will transform it all into projects with specific results. This is where all your dreams will begin to become part of your reality, and where your passion will ignite your dreams.

Real People: The Carters

The Carters began to see the possibilities as soon as they made their commitment to sell the retail computer store and pursue their dreams. First, they realized they could have a whole new consulting business serving clients with whom they had done business before. Second, they determined that their retail business could be sold to someone who would continue to serve their previous customers. Third, the new owner agreed to refer to the Carters retail customers who needed consultation about purchases made at the store.

In other words, they took their dream to a new level by evolving a new relationship. Rather than separating themselves completely from their previous business, they found a way to make a profitable connection for their new business.

Wasn't this coming year a great year?

Of course, there were some obstacles to overcome. The Carters had many attitudes and beliefs about closing the store: they couldn't see how they were going to continue serving their clients. They thought that closing the store meant they had failed. Changing your mind, or even failing at a dream, does not mean you are a failure.

Once they went through their process, they were able to turn their negative attitudes and beliefs around, and use them to propel themselves toward their dream. When they knew with clarity what they wanted, and that they were committed to having it, the next steps became evident: they scheduled the closing of the store, they set a date by which the new business would be set up, and they got into action. Setting the date made the commitment tangible and moved their dream into the project phase, the subject of the next chapter.

All that we see or seem
is but a dream within a dream.
— **EDGAR ALLAN POE**

CHAPTER 10

Projects That
Move You Forward

**If you have built castles in the air,
your work need not be lost; that is where they should be.
Now put the foundations under them.**

— HENRY DAVID THOREAU

IN CHAPTER 4, YOU CHOSE a specific area of your life to work on to simplify the process of learning the techniques in this book. You've been developing your dream in that area, going up the Passion Pyramid, opening up more and more possibilities about your dream. In this chapter, you will learn how to turn your dream into a project with specific, measurable results. The action of doing so will make your dream begin to exist in your life, not just in your head or on paper.

Remember that everything comes from Purpose. Standing in your Purpose, ask, with respect to the area you selected, "What dream do I have that I can turn into an exciting project?" Then look for what needs to be added to your project to get it scheduled into your life—a date, a person, and a number.

For instance, if your dream is to travel, your project might be to go on a vacation this year. If you don't yet know where you want to go, but you know the locale you want is exotic, open an atlas, pick a specific place and begin to arrange your trip.

Dreams come alive through projects
with specific and measurable results.

My own Life's Purpose is to joyously self-express and my personal dream is to travel the world in style and elegance; my project is to book an exotic cruise by a specific date.

Of course, there are many ways to travel the world in style and elegance. Other projects that could come from my Purpose and my dream might be to travel first class five times this year; to attend at least three formal events in cities outside my home town; to fly in a private jet plane at least once during the next six months; to spend three months in a foreign country living in a beautiful place.

You don't have to limit yourself to one project; all you have to do is make sure that your projects move you forward on your dream. When I develop projects for my professional dream—integrating more play time into my work—I can change things around, as long as everything remains aligned with my Purpose and my professional dream. Thus, I might create a project which would allow me to continue my work while taking in the California scenery. Note that I only have to create the project at this point; I don't have to limit the possibilities by figuring out how I'm going to do it. Sometimes, going to strategy too soon can kill your passion. We'll get to the planning process shortly.

Ellen, whose Purpose was to have a life filled with fun and adventure, had a well-being goal called, "To Live a Spa Life." She created a project called, "Go To An Elegant Spa At Least Four Times A Year, Each Time For At Least One Week's Duration." She didn't yet have any of it planned—financially, logistically, or time-wise—but once she created the project, it took on life and became part of her reality.

Some projects are easy; you merely have to schedule them into your calendar: to get into action on her dream, Ellen developed a simple project to get two facials and two massages each month. Since I too love the idea of a "spa life," I was inspired by her dream and adopted it as one of my own. I now lead one of my Dream University® retreats at a world class spa. You can join me for hiking, facials, massages and in depth dream work.

If you want your dreams to come true,
don't sleep.
— YIDDISH PROVERB

Some projects can be just that simple while others are complicated, and require a well-thought out plan to get there. A project has to be specific, but it can deal with any aspect of your life: Brian created a plan to raise $25,000 so his company could open for business in a big way. The only criterion for a project is that it come from the bottom up on the Passion Pyramid—meaning that it's an expression of your Purpose and your dream—and that it be specific and measurable.

Synchronicity

Synchronicity may be a fun, new way for you to think about having your dream. Before reading this book, you may have thought about your dream as something you might—or might not—ever have. Now, you've expanded your possibilities and allowed for more opportunities to create projects for reaching your dream. I gave a speech in Madrid to the Young Presidents' Organization. At the end of my talk a lovely woman with a beautiful European accent asked me to share one of my dreams with her. I thought to myself, "Take a risk. There must be an opportunity at hand." I told her that my dream was to spend the summer in Greece writing a novel. She opened her purse and handed me a business card saying, "I have a villa in Crete and it's empty all summer. Please come as my guest." And I will. Every day, my belief that magic happens when you share your dream, is validated.

When you look at the whole picture of your dream, you will see that some of the areas may overlap providing shortcuts. Or the overlap will enable you to handle something in one area of your life that automatically takes care of something in another area. This is called synchronicity: when things start to happen at the right time, when they flow together easily and work interchangeably. This is synchronicity, which creates ease. In order to have more of this, practice integrity. Say what you mean and mean what you say, and trust that you can easily have your dreams come true.

People will call me and say, "I followed the process, I did all the steps, but I keep having setbacks." When I ask them about their life, their relationships, their agreements with others and themselves, often there is evidence that they are saying one thing, yet doing another. Everything we say, do, think, feel and are, affects everything we want and have. Notice how you are in your life. Perhaps take a personal inventory and pay extra attention to what you are saying and doing. When we have integrity life seems to just ebb and flow and we have greater ease. If life is taking you on a bumpy ride it may be a message to check in and see how you are living.

If you stand in your Purpose and look at the broad picture of your dream, it's possible to get what you want while simplifying your life. New possibilities will become available as you develop projects and get into action on them. Opportunities that you couldn't have seen before will start to look like they have potential. Of course an old attitude or belief might stymie you. If this happens, ask yourself whether you're still committed to your dreams; if the answer is "Yes," do something, take some small step to demonstrate your commitment.

Synchronicity:

when things start to happen at the right time,

flow together easily

and work interchangeably.

You have no idea what could be waiting for you right around the bend, on the other side of the place where you got stuck. As long as your projects come from your Purpose and are aligned with your dreams, as long as you still feel the passion, stay in action.

Throughout this book, for the sake of simplicity, we have focused on your dreams in one area of your life. However, the intention of the process is that you will master the techniques of consciously designing your entire life. Once you learn the procedure—and you can only learn it by practicing—you'll find it easy to map it into all the other areas of your life.

I've cleared away tremendous clutter in my home and office. Mostly what remains in my office are my project files. As they grow, they open onto more projects, and sometimes-new projects develop within an existing one. There's a great deal of overlap because one of my dreams is to integrate my personal and professional life. That doesn't mean I'm a workaholic; it means that I've created work that expresses who I am in the world, and I can combine my work with the rest of my life, easily and joyfully.

Aligning Goals to Support Your Dream

Let's recap what you've accomplished thus far. Standing in your Purpose, you have created dreams in at least one aspect of your life.

You've stepped through the Sliding Glass Door and you're on the other side, where there is everything you're interested in or committed to having in your life. Now go back and have a look at the other areas of your life to ensure that they line up with your dream.

As you create a project, if you find a dream that seems inconsistent or incompatible—perhaps you're worried that you're selling out in one situation in order to have another—check to see whether your "concern" is real, or whether it's a negative attitude or belief. For example, if the hours you've designated for your project add up to more than 24 each day, you have an inconsistency. On the other hand, if they add up to six or eight and you're still troubled about having enough time for everything, acknowledge that the issue comes from an old belief. Then make a commitment that you will use your time in support of having your dream.

You have no idea

what could be waiting for you

right around the bend,

on the other side

of the place where you got stuck.

Look at your life holistically; all of the components, including the dreams, are—or need to be—working parts of your life. Get a picture of it as a whole; perhaps there's a piece that's missing, that would tie things together to give you more time and flexibility, to make your life easier.

During the Sliding Glass Door Exercise, one of my clients became very emotional. "I can't step through," she claimed.

When I asked why not, she explained there was no ground, no foundation. "Well, put it in," I said. What we imagine about our dreams can be very telling about what we are feeling. With the foundation in place, she could step through the door.

We later saw that her dream—to make some radical changes in her business—was a big stretch from where she was. When she realized the emotional difficulty her employees were having with her new plans, she began to lay the proper groundwork with them to make a smooth transition.

What are your visualizations and feelings telling you? What's missing from your life that, if in place, would make your life easier?

Align your dreams by eliminating any inconsistencies.

I'm not torn between my personal and professional aspects; they are both me. I give myself plenty of time to relax and play, so when I go away on vacation I often do it in a barter situation: perhaps I offer a workshop in exchange for a week at a health spa. Trading my services takes into consideration many of my dreams: my professional dream of having work that I love and that expresses who I am in the world; my personal dream of being with creative visionaries to produce results that have an impact; my well-being dream of being emotionally, mentally, spiritually, and physically balanced. The bartering opportunities never existed before I became clear about what I wanted and what I was committed to; now it exists regularly, and it ties together many of the aspects of my life.

A question that often comes up is how you identify the area you may have missed, the very one that may give you the complete arsenal of tools you need to make your dreams come true. Go back to the Passion Pyramid and look at your Life's Purpose. Then look at all the dreams you have determined you want in every aspect of your life. Ask yourself, "What would make my life easier; what would make my life take on a glow, what would give me more time, more fun, more excitement?"

This is not an exercise in creating more work for yourself. Rather, by asking yourself during the alignment process what you may not have seen before as a possibility, you will simplify your life and allow yourself to see new possibilities now. A growing number of people finds that what's missing are not necessarily tangible; they need more space, more time, or some other personal resource.

What would make your life easier?
What would make your life
take on a glow?
What would give you more time,
more fun, more excitement?

You don't necessarily have to create another project to accomplish these things; perhaps you can save yourself time and energy by linking together two or more of the projects you've already identified. Think positively; you are designing a new life for yourself. Rather than formulating a dream that's stated in the negative, such as "Remove some of the clutter," develop instead a dream that supports your having more space or time, freedom or flexibility.

Do you want to be more relaxed because you will feel better if you stop taking it all so seriously?

Did you leave out enough recreational time, or time simply to breathe and to be?

Is there a volunteer effort, or another contribution you want to make?

Are you making space in your life for what you want?

Years ago, I discovered that what was missing for me was to have work that I love. Just plugging that one piece into my dream enabled me to begin developing projects that I savor. For example, it had never occurred to me before that going on a cruise or to a spa was a way of making money or being successful in business. That possibility showed up when I included the element of having work that I love, and saw that I could tie it together with my other dreams. Recently on a book tour, while in Buffalo, New York I visited Niagara Falls and in Cincinnati I purchased a last minute ticket to a touring Broadway show. With a little effort, I can have fun wherever I go, and not have my life be just about "work or no work." I realized that I could flourish and take better care of myself while spending less time and energy than I had before, and that I could take time to play.

The more of yourself that you have, the more you can put into your projects, which are a way for you to project your dreams into the world. Schedule time for your dreams, and for the things that make you happy.

You can be doing work that you love to do.

Stretch Yourself

If you want to live every day with passion, design a project that's bigger than your life, one that you don't know how to accomplish. Don't create a project "out of the blue;" develop one out of your Purpose as you would any other project. My bigger-than-life project is that, by the time I die, people will be speaking about dreams in a completely new way, as if their dreams are something that absolutely can

The Passion Pyramid

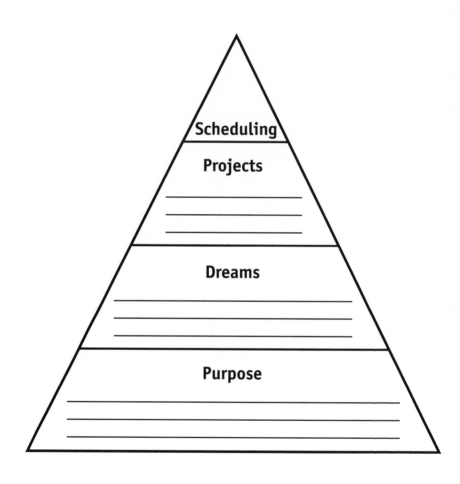

be had by a specific day. When you speak to me about your dreams, be prepared to pull out your calendar. I'm interested in getting you into action to make your dreams come true.

I'm not yet certain how to fulfill my bigger-than-life project, but it turns me on and gets me into conversation with extraordinary people. Remember, my dream is to partner with creative visionaries to produce impactful results. Speaking with people about their dreams allows everyone to show up as a visionary, to be turned on and excited about their ideas.

I don't allow myself to be stopped by the fact that I haven't figured out how to accomplish my bigger-than-life project. I move on by developing strategies and steps, by scheduling it into my life, and letting life happen. And it does.

To keep yourself updated on your progress moving up the Passion Pyramid, re-enter your Purpose, rewrite your dream, and indicate in the designated area on the Pyramid the project you created during this chapter. Make sure you are excited about your project and the possibilities it provides.

Remember your Purpose is what turns you on; from that you created dreams that fulfill your Purpose; then you developed a project or several projects that will get you going on your dream. Check in by rating yourself on the Passion Scale.

If you have created something that doesn't turn you on, change it. Develop a different project. If it all lines up and you're excited, even a little nervous about how you're going to make it happen, let's move on to doing it!

PASSION SCALE

Place an X next to the area that best describes your level of passion about your project. Do it right now.

____ RED HOT
____ TURNED ON
____ EXCITED
____ VERY INTERESTED
____ INTERESTED
____ SOME POSSIBILITY
____ NO INTEREST

CHAPTER 11

Strategies and Steps— Being In Action

Divide and conquer.

— CHINESE PROVERB

NOW THAT YOU KNOW what your project is, all you have to do is figure out how you're going to make it happen! There are multiple ways of completing any project or achieving any end result. To make your project part of your reality, you will need strategies and steps to guide you toward your dream.

Some of us are great dreamers, but a little lacking in the strategy department. And some of us are brilliant strategists, but need a little practice dreaming. I think we should pump up both muscles, both sides of our brain. Let's dream and imagine and be practical and strategic. Let's dream and make our dreams come true.

A strategy is the approach or plan you will take to actually achieve your dream. Tactics are the specific step-by-step items to accomplish the strategy. Sometimes, when an entire project is put on a "To Do" list, the project is actually composed of four or five separate tactics; if the separate tasks aren't listed individually, the project may never happen. As a matter of fact, the number one way dreams die is that we put them on a "To Do" list. They must be broken down into small steps before they are scheduled, steps that can be easily accomplished, or you'll probably never get to them. When you get clear about the project, as you did in the last chapter, you can explore the strategies and steps you will need to accomplish it.

For example, I decided to create a project called, "Go On At Least One Free and Fun Cruise To An Exotic Place Within The Next Three Months." Then I listed the ways I could make it happen.

In this case, I couldn't have chosen to purchase a ticket for a cruise, because my project was to go on a free cruise. It's important to be clear about what you want. One set of strategies might be needed to go on a fun cruise, while a different set is required to go on a free and fun cruise.

Other strategies I could have chosen include finding someone who would pay for my trip, or entering a contest to win a free cruise. I chose to create a bartering relationship by booking my workshop on a cruise ship in return for a free trip.

The steps to accomplish the strategy were clear: list and describe some topics about which I could speak; prepare a biography; get the name and number of several cruise ship lines, which might be interested in such an arrangement. I decided to focus my energy on a certain cruise ship, rather than mass-mailing my proposal: I wanted the best cruise I could find, so I committed to getting booked by Cunard Lines, which owns the luxury liner, Queen Elizabeth II.

Because I was passionate about what I was doing, I was feeling powerful about accomplishing the results. I was definitely in action. In a period of three weeks, I developed promotional materials, had a photo made, sent out a package, and scheduled a date by which I wanted to set sail. Before I had a chance to make a follow-up call to see if they were interested, they called me. I was booked to go on the cruise five months ahead of what I had scheduled.

**A man's real worth is determined
by what he does when he has nothing to do.
— MEGIDDO MESSAGE**

If I can make this kind of thing happen, so can you. On the following pages you will find forms you can use to develop the strategies and steps you will need to create your own projects and make your dreams come true. Follow the simple "designing a blueprint" directions and walk through the process.

Designing A Blueprint

Here is a formula for getting into action on any project.
1. Outline or overview what's needed using the Strategies Section.
2. Identify your resources. Be creative.
3. Break the steps into single items to do.
4. Add dates and resources.
5. Put in chronological order on the Scheduling page.
6. See where you are overscheduled and where you can reschedule.
7. Be in action on your dream every day or at least every week.

Being Resourceful

A crucial component of creating successful strategies and steps is making use of the resources in all the areas of your life. On the facing page you will find a form you can use to write out who and what are your resources. Think about the people you know in the different aspects of your life; consider what's available to you in the way of technology and information. There's nothing that's not a potential resource. Your list may not be long, but it will be a way for you to leverage what you already have.

I'm an advocate of simplification and short cuts. If you can find a faster way of getting something done, do it. One of your strategies might be to accomplish something that you don't know how to do, and one of your tactics might be to learn it. However, another approach might be to hire or partner with somebody who already has that knowledge. By getting clear about your resources, you can cross reference them with your dreams and projects, and determine how things might come together.

Strategies and steps do go hand in hand, as illustrated in Brian's example at the end of this chapter. When you develop your list of strategies and steps, code them in a way that tells you at a glance what you have to do to accomplish them:

"S" means all you have to do is schedule them.

"B" means the strategy or step is a way for you to "be," rather than something you have to do.

"P" means the strategy or step needs a plan to develop it further so that it can be scheduled into your calendar.

"D" is my favorite letter, because it means "Done." It's wonderful when you can see what you've accomplished and that you're moving forward on your project.

Strategies and Steps:
A Road Map for Getting There

STRATEGIES: YOUR APPROACH TO ACHIEVING YOUR DREAM

1. _____

2. _____

3. _____

4. _____

5. _____

STEPS: YOUR "TO DO" LIST
(complete for each of the strategies you list above)

DATE	ITEM	RESOURCE
_____	_____	_____
_____	_____	_____
_____	_____	_____
_____	_____	_____
_____	_____	_____
_____	_____	_____
_____	_____	_____

SCHEDULING: Put the "items to do" in chronological order and transfer them to your calendar.

Month _____

Day _____   To do   _____

_____   _____

_____   _____

_____   _____

Month _____

Day _____   To do   _____

_____   _____

_____   _____

_____   _____

Month _____

Day _____   To do   _____

_____   _____

_____   _____

_____   _____

When you get to this stage, it's important to differentiate between a project and a specific step. It's a lot easier to get into action on a single step than it is on a whole project. You know that old joke, "How do you eat an elephant?" "A bite at a time." That's how you will accomplish your project, one manageable bite at a time.

My Resources

PEOPLE AND ORGANIZATIONS WHO CAN HELP ME:

Friends Who Can Help Me:_____

_____

Friends of Friends Who Can Help Me: _____

_____

Family Members Who Can Help Me:_____

_____

Business Associates Who Can Help Me:_____

_____

Organizations or Associations That Can Help Me:_____

_____

Who Will Support Me? _____

_____

Who Can Advise Me? _____

_____

Who Can Really Help Me? _____

_____

People I Don't Know Who Can Help Me: _____

_____

Who Is The One Person Who Won't Help Me: _____

_____

How Can I Use Even The Person Who Won't Help? _____

_____

THINGS I CAN DO TO MAKE MY DREAM COME TRUE:

Places I Can Go: _____

_____

Things I Can Read: _____

_____

New Things I Can Try: _____

_____

Old Things I Can Reference: _____

_____

The One Place I Know I Can't Get Any Help: _____

_____

How Can I Use This? _____

_____

The Dream Bank Deposit Slip

When you are looking for people who are committed to encouraging the possibilities in your life and to supporting your dreams, remember me. I'm one of those people. I believe that every aspect of all your dreams can come true, and I've created The Dream Bank, where you can deposit your dream with me.

On the facing page you will find a Dream Bank Deposit Slip. I invite you to fill in all the information requested; then, where it says, "My dream is _____ ," write out your dream and commit to an action step you will take within this next week. Get into action right away by creating a step and scheduling the date.

I recommend you create a "WOW." *Within One Week*, what's an action step you will take to move your dream forward? Make it simple and set yourself up for an easy win, a success.

Here are some of the dreams and *WOW*'s that I've received.

My dream is:

> To have my pilot's license, and *Within One Week*, I completed my first solo flight.

> To open a retreat center, and *WOW* (*Within One Week*), I began to scout international locations.

> To invent and launch a new product, *WOW* I mapped out a strategy and had a team in place.
> To be in a loving committed relationship, *WOW* I ran a personal ad and had 2 fun dates.
> To have new fun experiences every day, *WOW* I renewed passion in my marriage.
> To produce a nationally syndicated TV show, *WOW* I met with 3 cable stations.
> To retire, *WOW* I mapped out a transition plan with my business partner.
> To sing again (ex-Metropolitan Opera star), *WOW* I was singing again.
> To triple my income, *WOW* I had my husband's support and a new Team started.
> To spend time reconnecting with my family, *WOW* I booked a family vacation.

Dream Bank Deposit Slip

My dream is _____

_____

My WOW (Within One Week) is:_____

Name:_____

Address: _____

_____

Phone: (Home)_____ (Office) _____

Email:_____

When you have completed your Deposit Slip, photocopy the page, and send it to by mail or email. My contact information is in the back of this book. When I receive it you'll become part of a global network, a DreamTeam for people all over the world with all kinds of dreams.

If you choose not to send it to my Dreams Bank, fill in the deposit slip and tape it to your mirror, or put it in another place where you'll read it daily. It's powerful, however, to have your dreams registered with someone who believes they can come true. I'll be that person for you; I believe in you and in your having what you want.

Is it both exciting and confronting to commit to an action step? Of course, and hopefully it will be a positive and important step. Read about Judy and how when she filled out her Dream Bank Deposit Slip, she became angry. All kinds of limiting beliefs came up. But committing to an action item, and taking that first step was a life changing experience for her.

Real People: Judy

Judy was a talented singer and performer, but decided early in her career to postpone her music dreams and marry a wonderful man. Although she sang in church choir, her main focus in life was to be a great wife and mom. Her family and home were her first priority. She was grateful that she could provide marketing services for Tony Orlando in the town of Branson, Missouri, where she lived. But as she went through this dream process, there was no denying that she was a singer at heart, although it was a well kept secret, especially from Tony.

On her Dream Bank Deposit Slip, her WOW, within one-week commitment was that at age 44, she would set up an audition with her friend and music producer Norman Berger, who sang with the Tokens and arranged the original version of The Lion Sleeps Tonight.

Immediately she got quite upset because she didn't see how it could happen. Judy's life had been dedicated to others and the thought of pursuing her own dream felt overwhelming, frustrating, and even impossible. Casey, her daughter asked her what was going on and with great insight this eighteen year old said, "Mom, I'm grown up. I release you to pursue your dreams." It's no wonder why shortly after this, Casey went on to win Miss American Teen. She continues to be a great Dream-Team member for her mom.

Judy's life changed there, but remember, it started by her writing her dream and action step, and then sharing it. Within one week, she called Norman. They wound up going into a studio and half way through the first song, he turned to the technician and said, "She needs to do an album." On her wedding anniversary that year, her husband Rob took her into the studio and with some of the members of Tony Orlando's band she recorded *May the Circle Be Unbroken*. What a great DreamTeam song. And shortly after that, Judy sold several of her original country songs to up and coming artists.

There was one more piece. Judy showed up many nights in the audience of Tony's shows. Since she had worked for him, he was always glad to see her, but had no idea that she had this amazing gift and talent.

Most nights, he would walk out into the audience and hand the microphone to various people inviting them to sing a bit. When Judy motioned for him to give her the mike, he was surprised and a little confused, but only for a moment. Her singing stopped him in his tracks. She later told him she had a dream and wanted his help. She made a very specific request. "I want to be in your show. Can I?" Opening night of his Christmas show, "Santa & Me" it happened. Tony said to Judy, "You, every show, starting tomorrow."

Real People: Brian

Brian, the man who wanted to start a new company, decided that, to open for business, one of his strategies was to find office space. The steps he chose were to look at a certain number of spaces by a specific date, to review his resources, to speak with other companies about sharing space, and to be in a new office within a certain time frame. The most powerful step of all was that he committed himself to a specific date and wrote it on his calendar.

Register your dreams with someone who believes that they can come true.

There were many other strategies that Brian developed so that he could open for business, including having the necessary office equipment, producing the marketing and promotional materials, setting up an accounting system, preparing a strategic plan for his board of directors, enlisting key people to support his vision, and raising funds. Under the area of money, Brian's tactics were to break down his operating income: by a certain date he would know what his expenses would be, and he would then identify resources for financing. To simplify his pursuit he broke down even those specifics into additional strategies and steps. By breaking all his strategies down into specific items to do, Brian successfully accomplished his project and his dream, a step at a time.

It's a lot easier to get into action on a step than it is on a whole project.

CHAPTER 12

Playing on a
Winning DreamTeam

**A burning purpose attracts others
who are drawn along with it and help fulfill it.**

— MARGARET BOURKE-WHITE

SOME PEOPLE STILL HARBOR old beliefs that they have to do everything themselves. Perhaps it's that old John Wayne-type, individualistic, American frontier attitude. If you feel that standing on your own two feet means never accepting help from anyone, it's important to acknowledge the tendency. Of course, you *can* "go it alone" if you insist, but it's a longer, harder process.

I caution you, however, not to take on everything by yourself. You want to simplify the journey to having your dream, not complicate it. If you're part of a winning team, you can accelerate progress and expand your horizons—in short, it's easier and faster to do it with other people.

When I speak of a winning DreamTeam, I don't necessarily mean a club or a group of people that meets with regularity. A formal group has potential for some people and not for others. Rather, I think of a winning team as a resource group, people to whom you can turn when you need advice, when you need a sounding board, when you need to unravel a thorny problem, or when you need someone to listen.

Although we all tend not to want to bother others or to recruit assistance, what happens whenever two or more are gathered is uncanny. I personally believe you're only a few phone calls away from anyone in the world that you need to contact. Use this to your advantage.

You want to simplify

the journey to having your dream,

not complicate it.

Letting others help you is a form of true generosity, because you enable them to feel good about contributing to your success. Many people love to make a difference by helping others. You can allow people to assist you most effectively by learning how to make powerful requests. Get clear about what you need, find the individuals who can help you get it, and ask for what you want.

One of the tools you can use to decide what skills you need on your team is to develop written criteria. On the facing page, list your requirements for the members of your winning team.

Enrolling Others: Your Current Resources

There are many reasons why others would be interested in participating with you. After all, you're a go-getter with a big dream; in its completion, your dream might benefit others. What happens out of enrollment is beyond anything you can imagine. Invite people to be on your DreamTeam, and here's a tip. Make specific requests and make it easy for them to say yes, like Judy did with Tony Orlando.

For example, one of my dreams was to be out in the world speaking about something in which I believe. I shared my dream and connected, through a friend-of-a-friend, with someone who was director of creative services for a national television network. The network person eventually scheduled me on a nationwide talk show, something that never would have happened if I had not been speaking about my dream.

CRITERIA FOR MEMBERS OF YOUR WINNING DREAMTEAM

Skills: _____

_____

_____

Interests: _____

_____

_____

Education: _____

_____

_____

Resources: _____

_____

_____

Other: _____

_____

_____

_____

With whom should you speak? Begin by reviewing the Resources forms completed in chapter 11, to see who's available in your current world to help. Start talking to those people about your dream. Tell them what it is you're committed to; help them to experience your excitement by sharing your enthusiasm with them.

Then ask your resources who else they know. Remember, you're only one phone call away from somebody you need to reach, two at the most. By asking those you know to name others, you are developing a network. Before long, you will have clarified your needs and you'll start to understand who you want on your team. Find at least one person who believe in your dreams, and sometimes the "more the merrier."

You know some people right now who can fill spots on your team immediately, and you'll find others during the process. If you need a confidante, someone to whom you can tell all your secrets, look around among your resources; that person may already exist. If someone with business savvy does not exist among your current resources, find out if anyone you know is acquainted with such a person; if not, go out and find the individuals with the skills you need.

Enrolling Others: New Resources

Your team need not be composed only of people who are currently on your Resource List. When you need additional skills on the team, add new members who are outside of your immediate universe.

The people you need

to help you make your dream come true

are everywhere, and within your reach.

You can find new people with the skills you need by identifying groups and associations to which they may belong. Several directories list organizations by subject area: for example, Gale's Encyclopedia of Associations, or the National Trade and Professional Associations of the United States. Ask people you already know what associations they belong to; look in the business section of your local newspaper to identify groups that meet in your area.

Plan to attend group meetings as a non-member, go with your Purpose in mind, and be clear about the intended result. Decide in advance what kind of people you want to meet there, what you want to get out of the meeting, and what you want to communicate. Once you're there, you have an opportunity to develop relationships with all kinds of new people; plan to participate and interact with them. Always speak your dream.

Most people who attend such gatherings may shake a few hands, talk with one or two individuals, and then leave. You are not such a person, because you know the power of sharing your dream in a new group. You are now clear about your dream and can articulate it with clarity and passion. Talk about your dream from the moment you walk into the room, and they will see you as a dynamic individual, committed to making your dream a reality.

You start with a blank slate among new people; capture the energy and input from those encounters. If you notice that someone is getting excited about your dream, ask how that individual would like to participate. Make it easy for them to say yes.

It is also powerful to ask others about their commitment to their own dream. As they speak, you might discover a way to join with them and further your vision. For instance, someone who's committed to literacy might be able to help you fulfill your dream of creating more jobs for people. Perhaps together you can find employment for previously unemployable people who have learned how to read. By listening to other people's dreams, you can hear about new possibilities, get new ideas and find new resources.

**Many ideas grow better when
transplanted into another mind,
than in the one where they sprang up.**
— JUSTICE OLIVER WENDELL HOLMES, JR.

Another way to enroll people onto your winning team is to become an active letter writer. Whenever someone who can further your dream is mentioned in a book or an article, or is featured on radio or television, note how to contact the publication or the station. Take a risk; write a letter, and tell that individual about your dream.

Perhaps you will be attending a convention featuring a speaker you'd like to have as part of your network. Write in advance and say how much you look forward to the presentation. While you're at the meeting, approach that person and introduce yourself; then write a quick follow-up letter when the meeting is over. These simple steps will take you little time and yield big results. By doing them you will have made yourself part of that new person's consciousness and, in the months that follow, you can begin a dialogue in person.

Don't be afraid to call people on the phone. If you're not sure exactly what you want to say, write out a couple of points and keep them in front of you, or practice speaking to somebody else. You would be amazed at who answers their own phone and how accessible many people can be. Be prepared. Have a clear intention and be respectful of their time. Remember why you are calling them and make a specific request. My experience is most people would like to say yes and be helpful, if they can.

Action makes more fortunes than caution.
— VAUVENARGUES

Jeff Davidson, in his popular book *Blow Your Own Horn: How to Get Noticed—And Get Ahead*, suggests that you think about the ten people you need to call right now. Perhaps they include an association director, a magazine editor, or someone in another industry. You will find the task is less formidable if you break it down into its individual components. First, compile a list of the phone numbers and have them in front of you. Then commit to making a specific number of calls each day. Get into action.

Look for resources in your own company.

With whom can you speak about your dream when you go to work tomorrow morning?

Is your boss enrolled, or any of your co-workers?

Do they even know that you have a dream?

Have you already decided that they're not potential partners and they can't help you? Or are you sitting there thinking that you can't pursue your dream without your boss's support, even though your boss may not know what your dream is? Don't kill off possibilities before you've explored them.

Look for ways to share your dream and tie it into the other aspects of your life. It's essential that you enroll your family in your dream by communicating what you want. Let them hear your commitment and enthusiasm, and be unstoppable regardless of how they respond.

WHO ARE THE TEN PEOPLE YOU KNOW YOU NEED TO CALL?

1. _____

2. _____

3. _____

4. _____

5. _____

6. _____

7. _____

8. _____

9. _____

10. _____

Demonstrate your commitment by taking action. There really is no other way. As they see your commitment, no matter how big the dream may be, eventually they will stand behind you. Tenacity often yields credibility. Show them you're not giving up; ask them to support you, even if it's only by believing in you, and be open to receiving their support.

Sometimes we feel absolutely sure that we cannot get the support we want from the people we want it most. Let them change their minds. Any day, any moment could be the moment they sign up to be on your team.

When you think about involving your family, notice your attitudes and beliefs. Is that voice inside your head saying, "My parents never thought I could do it" or "The family will think I'm off on another hair-brained scheme"? Those are just your attitudes and beliefs; you can go back and write them in the attitudes and beliefs section in chapter 6, but you don't have to include them in what you are designing for the future.

Be clear about what you're committed to, and start to speak it powerfully so that people around you can help. Get others on board, whether they play an intimate role in your dream or a tangential one. It's all part of building a winning team.

The Members of Your Winning DreamTeam

One of the ways to engage others quickly is to make a request. Ask for something specific; the more precise the request, the more specific the response. Simply say, "I'd like to make a request of you." Your query can be accepted or declined, or the other person can make a counter-offer. When you make a request, be willing to hear what people say in response.

Tenacity often yields credibility.

When you ask for something, you signal to others that your interest in what they have to offer is more than casual. They are likely to take you more seriously. You convey the message that you'd like to have an answer, that you're interested in moving the conversation and, possibly, the relationship forward.

Once you've got someone's attention, you can enlist his or her services in several ways. One of my favorite methods is to trade services. One woman I know conducts public relations activities for her certified public accountant in exchange for accounting assistance. Someone else trades strategic planning services for massage therapy, or coaching for cooking.

If you think you don't have anything to barter, re-examine what you're passionate about. Most of us can offer some kind of service they can exchange for another. It's a great way of experiencing what you're capable of doing.

The Skills On Your Team

There are many kinds of skills you will need on your winning team, although you can expect your needs to change over time. As you develop new projects and complete old ones, you may find yourself in need of talents you did not consider important earlier. However, there are three kinds of people you will always need on your team: mentors, coaches, and partners.

<u>Mentors:</u> People who "know the ropes" are an invaluable asset. The skills required of a mentor are perhaps the easiest to define, and the easiest to find. If you are looking for someone who can teach you

how to move forward quickly, or how to create short cuts, or how to break into a new area you're interested in, you need only seek someone with expertise in the field.

A lawyer, for example, can mentor another; a woman who runs her own established business can guide an entrepreneur who is starting out; an experienced writer can assist a fledgling author. Look for someone who has been where you want to go, is still learning and growing, and is happy to share those experiences with you.

Mentors— _____

_____

Coaches— _____

_____

Partners— _____

_____

<u>Coaches:</u> A Dream Coach is someone who listens for what's possible, helps you break through when you're stuck, and holds you accountable for doing what you said you were going to do. The coaching concept has really caught on and there are lots of trained professionals available for hire, some perhaps right in your backyard. Check out our website to find the perfect Dream Coach for you.

Although I am no longer available for one-on-one sessions, I do invite you to join me at a live Dream University® event where we can work together in an intimate setting. Or through our online courses I can walk you through my process in detail and at your own speed. There's information on both in the back of this book.

You can employ a strategic planner or a marketing specialist; or you can train a close friend to take your dreams seriously and support you in your efforts. You can be there for each other. Look for someone with qualities you admire: strength of character, clarity of vision, commitment, dependability. Once you identify your coach, design the coaching relationship using some or all of the questions on the facing page.

In what area do you want to be coached?

What is the specific, measurable result that you want?

What is your weekly campaign of activities?

How often will you and your coach speak?

For what length of time?

How do you want to be coached?

Do you want to know when you're doing it right and wrong?

Are you going to be open to hearing criticism as "coaching," or will you hear it as judgment?

Partners: Partners are people who will give, receive, and share equally with you as members of your winning team. You can develop partnerships with individuals who are already in your life—family members, friends, business associates—or with organizations and groups of individuals. When you know what result you want from a partner on your team, seek out candidates. Sometimes simply picking up the phone and having a conversation with someone might initiate something new. A project is the glue that will allow you and your partner to work together. Design a venture you're both clear about, with specific, measurable results; out of that, the partnership will develop.

As you review the list of resources, you might notice that there are dozens of people in your life of whom you never thought to make a request, or unique combinations of individuals whom you never before thought of putting together.

You won't want to feel overwhelmed, however, about where you'll find the time for new ventures. If you're creating your winning team on track, everything you do will support your Purpose, enhance your dreams, and be filled with passion. That's always your touchstone for making sure that you're on target toward making your dream come true.

It's rare that I come across a dream or project that wouldn't benefit from a team. I'm also often asked my skeptics, "Can you really design a strategy for any dream, even finding a new relationship? Read about Gwen and the team she assembled around her dream to meet a man. My shortcut strategy for meeting new potential relationship candidates is "flirt. What I mean is, be friendly. Experience shows that we are all waiting for the other person to initiate conversation.

I once made an overture to a very powerful and successful man. As our relationship flourished he told me that we would have never gotten together had I not made the first move. Although he is comfortable talking to thousands of people, heads of states and Presidents, he feels awkward starting a conversation with a woman. Unbelievable perhaps, yet true.

Real People: Gwen

Gwen's professional life was sailing along, but by the time she hit her late 30's there was a new dream that was taking precedent. She wanted to be in a loving relationship with her dream man and have a family. She realized for this to happen she needed to share her dream and build a solid DreamTeam who would help her.

She went "on line" and sent out a great email to twenty of her friends and associates. It said this, "I am sending you this note with three specific requests:

1. Will you be on my DreamTeam? (Yes means you will hold my dream in your heart and check in with me to see that I am taking action on my dream).

2. Please read my vision of the kind of relationship that I am seeking and the qualities of a man that I desire.

3. Please introduce me to any and all eligible bachelors that you believe are potential candidates for a match with me. I trust you."

Her email went on to include her wish list and closed by saying this, "The more I voice who I am, what I am seeking, and what I love, the sooner I will have what my heart desires." Her friends responded very supportively (always the sign of true friends). They told her they thought this was a bold move and they would help her. Gwen has been having lots of dates and continues to share her dream. I just called her for an update and she said there is now a new man in her life. You can create a DreamTeam to help achieve any dream you may have. Use your resources. Also, the Internet can be the ultimate Dream Machine.

The Goose Story

Next fall, when you see geese heading south for the winter ... flying along in V formation ... consider what science has discovered as to why they fly that way:

**As each bird flaps its wings, it creates
an uplift for the bird immediately following.
By flying in V formation, the whole flock adds
at least seventy-one percent greater flying range than
if each bird flew on its own.
People who share a common direction and sense of community
can get where they are going more quickly and easily
because they are travelling on the thrust of one another.
When a goose falls out of formation, it suddenly feels the drag
and resistance of trying to go it alone ... and quickly gets back into
formation to take advantage of the lifting power of the bird in front.
If we have as much sense as a goose we will stay in
formation with those who are headed the same way we are.
When the Head Goose gets tired, it rotates back
in the wing and another goose flies point.
It is sensible to take turns doing demanding jobs
with people or with geese flying south.
Geese honk from behind to encourage those up
front to keep up their speed.
What do we say when we honk from behind?**

Finally, and this is important,
when a goose gets sick or is wounded by gunshots and
falls out of formation, two other geese fall out with that goose
and follow it down to lend help and protection.
They stay with the fallen goose until it is able to fly,
or until it dies; and only then do they launch out on their own,
or with another formation to catch up with their group.
If we have the sense of a goose,
We will stand by each other like that.

— SOURCE UNKNOWN

CHAPTER 13

Communicating
Your Dream
as a Way of Living

**The difference between the right word
and the almost right word is the difference
between lightning and the lightning bug.**
— MARK TWAIN

YOU HAVE ASSEMBLED A WINNING TEAM, and you've become adept at attracting more and more people who are interested in what you're doing. To accelerate toward your dream, you will want to continue communicating successfully with your team, and with others as well.

The members of your team need to hear you speak about your dream, or they won't know how they can help you. You might feel a little awkward at first, but the more you articulate your dream, the more powerful you'll become. Like anything else, it requires practice.

In today's world, people are inundated by enormous amounts of information competing for their attention. For example, in 1968, the portion of a statement or speech used for television news, called a "soundbite," ran an average of 42 seconds. By 1988, soundbites were down to 9.8 seconds. And with the addition of the Internet, we enter the 21st century in information overload.

In other words, you have less than ten seconds to speak your dream; that's about how much time you have for someone to understand what you're trying to do. If you want to break through the information din, practice saying what you want to say, and see if you can get it across clearly and comfortably in ten seconds.

The ten-second exercise may surprise you. In fact, you can complete three sentences within that amount of time. For example, the words you are reading in this paragraph can be said in about ten seconds.

On the previous page there is space to write your dream or your project in 25 words or less. Write it, practice speaking it aloud, and then practice by speaking it to other people. If others don't understand your message immediately, revise it until they do. Here are some examples of brief, distinct descriptions:

> I intend to contact and speak with 100 people about preservation of the rain forest, and to create a television series about it.

> I'm going to hold a one-day seminar for children of divorced parents.

> I will make available to all employees in the Washington, D.C.-area an effective program for retirement savings.

> I plan to invent the best relationship with a man that I can have.

> I will make my department the most successful in the company.

The expression of what you want can be simple or it can be sophisticated. Base your decision on the nature of the dream you're committed to creating. Mine is to have people speak about dreams in a new way, to believe that dreams are something they can have come true in their lifetime. What's yours?

An orator is a man who says
what he thinks and feels what he says.
— WILLIAM JENNINGS BRYAN

Communicating Your Dream

In 25 words or less, write in the space below a clear description of your dream or your project.

_____

_____

_____

_____

_____

_____

Now rate yourself on the Passion Scale. If you're not excited about your dream, others won't be either. Listen to yourself; hear how you sound. See how you feel. Tell us about your dream.

PASSION SCALE

Place an X next to the area that best describes your level of passion regarding speaking about your dream or project. Do it right now.

_____ RED HOT
_____ TURNED ON
_____ EXCITED
_____ VERY INTERESTED
_____ INTERESTED
_____ SOME POSSIBILITY
_____ NO INTEREST

Who's Listening?

When you tell people what your dream is, you will want to know whether they've heard you. Look into their eyes; are they confused or upset about what you're saying? Are they excited and "with you?" Do they understand? If you're not sure, stop and find out. Ask them what they think. If they're not excited about your dream, it doesn't mean that you did something wrong; it may not be the right dream for them. Perhaps they can still be your friends or business associates, but not people you want on your team.

Notice whose listening and how they're listening, and invite them to hear what you're saying in a way that's powerful. Remember that when *you* started to go for your dream, you had a variety of negative attitudes, beliefs, concerns and fears; others might also harbor attitudes that are limiting. People who care about you may feel especially convinced that you're going in the wrong direction, taking too much risk, or putting yourself in an unstable situation by breaking out of the norm.

Train people to listen to you. Explain what the word possibility means, and ask them to hear what's possible for *you*. Request that they suspend their automatic negative reactions and judgments, and that they hear your dream from your perspective.

You don't necessarily have to convince people to see things your way to receive their support. It may take them awhile before they're comfortable about accepting your dream. In the meantime, commit yourself to the possibility of getting their support in exactly the way you've asked for it. Believe that you can have that kind of a relationship, and keep speaking about your dream.

Notice who's listening to you
and how they're listening,
and train them to hear what you're saying
in a way that's powerful.

If you think it will overwhelm people, you may not want to speak all of your dream in one sitting. You can do it in stages; keep living and speaking what you want, and sharing it with others so they can experience what's going on for you. Eventually they will reach the stage at which, whether times are good or bad, you can share your dream completely.

Maybe everyone won't reach such a stage. At some point you may decide that a particular person won't fit on your DreamTeam. That happens sometimes, and it's good to know when you have enough information to make that decision. However, I encourage you not to write people off at the beginning if they don't align with your dream. Request that they react as you would like, and give them a chance to do so.

I know there are schools of thought that say you should not indiscriminately share your dreams and I respect that. But if you are not sharing your dreams with many people, you may be missing some wonderful and unexpected opportunities for help. Then of course, there are those negative people, the dream stealers or dream killers, to be aware of. One woman told me that her own mother is so negative that she stopped sharing her dreams with her. Then one day she had this insight. "If everything in life serves a function, I wonder what my mother's negative attitude could serve?" She got it. Whenever she is ready to launch a new product or service, she calls her mother. As expected, her mom tells her everything that could possibly go wrong. This woman then designs strategies to manage all those potential obstacles. She overcame her limiting belief about her mother's negativity and found a way to use and benefit from it.

When you share your dream, it's okay also to speak about your fears and concerns. If others are facing the same fears and concerns, the issues can be put on the table for discussion. You may recall that, in Chapter 6, we spoke of the importance of honesty about your current reality; sharing that truth with another person can be an insightful experience.

Part of the communications process involves dancing the dance of interaction. Trust, let the conversation flow, and listen to what is being said. Something new might show up: perhaps they know of a new resource; maybe they will suggest a new way for you to look at something. Don't be rigidly attached to what is already in your mind. In speaking your dream, new opportunities will show up. Keep your eyes and ears open. Expect success.

The story of Gillian appears below and illustrates the benefits of enrolling others. What's important about Gillian's tale is that a major international event started with somebody's dream. The vision became bigger and took on new form when Gillian began speaking her dream and enrolling others. All kinds of opportunities showed up, and different people became part of the winning team to make it a success.

This is an example of how a dream became a reality; how communication and sharing got people enrolled and excited; and how the dream became bigger and better than what any individual at first thought was possible.

Don't write people off automatically if,
at the beginning, they don't
align with your dream.
Request that they react as you would like,
and give them a chance to do so.

Real People: Gillian

Gillian was the head of the U.S. contingent of The World Association of Women Entrepreneurs. Her dream was to invite women from all over the world to Washington, D.C., where they would be treated in a special way.

Gillian spoke her dream to me and I became excited about it. Together, we organized a group of women to brainstorm around her idea. I came up with the dream. We would hold a major luncheon and international media event in the nation's capital at the National Press Club.

The objective of this event was to honor women entrepreneurs from thirty countries around the world, and to have them recognized by other women business owners, corporations, government officials, and by the media. The exposure and visibility was expected to garner greater national attention for the organization, additional funds, an increase in U.S. membership, and a boost to the organization's international membership.

As the brainstorming continued, we decided to create "The Declaration of International Partnership." We developed a document that focused on five areas in which women business owners could make an impact: education, environment, enterprise, communication, and innovation. Some 500 people attended the sell out event and you could hear a pin drop as each of the 30 country presidents signed the document. It was hailed as a historic event, and got major TV and print exposure, including the international edition of *USA Today*. And just for the record, there was no budget available for producing this stellar event. Funds were raised and corporate sponsors signed on because it was an amazing vision expressed with great passion. Every dream starts with an idea and grows proportionately to the amount of energy, excitement, and commitment behind it.

When you begin speaking your dream

and enrolling others,

your dream can get bigger

and take on new forms,

and all kinds of

opportunities will show up.

CHAPTER 14

Designing Your Environment

Two stonecutters were asked what they were doing.
The first said, "I'm cutting this stone into blocks."
The second replied, "I'm on a team that's building a cathedral."
— OLD STORY

ENROLLING OTHERS TO SUPPORT your dream is one important aspect of using resources. Another is designing your environment. As you progress on the path to making your dream come true, and you begin to realize that more and more is possible, additional opportunities and resources begin to become available. Whereas you may once have been concerned about not having any real possibilities, now you may feel overwhelmed by them.

The process is dynamic and ongoing. As you enroll people in your dream, you generate additional projects. As you take on other projects and develop new resources, you discover other people you wish to enroll. The new people lead you to new projects, and you find yourself constantly rearranging your physical and emotional environment to support your new endeavors.

The point of designing your environment is to create an atmosphere that will accommodate your changing needs while remaining clutter-free. You began the process way back in Chapter One, when you first started looking at your passion. That is, after all, the environment for which you are designing. Aligning your dreams with your Purpose—removing the inconsistencies—was just another way of removing clutter.

As you progress on the path

to making your dream come true,

you begin to realize

that more and more is possible.

You might start this phase of designing your environment with something as simple as cleaning off your desk or organizing a special room. At the end of this chapter, read more about Judy, the singer whose story you heard in Chapter 11, and how she made her dream real by setting up a space that would literally support her.

There are many books written about eliminating physical clutter; don't belabor it, do it so you will have space to continue creating and reaching for your dream. Similarly, if there are emotional issues keeping you from being clear about what your dream will look like, or about how you'll have the time to get it, clear them out of your way.

Finding Time

Time is a funny thing. Sometimes we feel that it's closing in around us; but when there's something we're passionate about, we create a way to make it happen. I wrote my book *Doing Less and Having More* primarily because I so often heard people say, "Not only do I not have time to make my dreams happen, I don't even have time to know what my dreams are." So I wrote a book that teaches how to make your life easier so you will have more time and greater ease.

Each of my project files has a list of strategies and steps—the items to do—attached to the front of it. If I'm in my office with an extra hour between calls, I can pull out one of my project files, do any item on the list, and I'm in action on something I love in my life. My projects are the mechanism for fulfilling my Life's Purpose. I spend most of my time working on my projects. At the end of the day or the week, when I want to plan ahead, I look at my project files and create the next week. This is the process, known as living by design, for actually creating a dream-come-true life. Learn to live more from your passion and less from your calendar, or better yet, fill your calendar with the steps for achieving your dreams.

It takes focus and commitment to design your whole life to work this way. It takes time, too, to learn a completely new way to live, think, and plan. Here's a little incentive. I have often seen people go farther in life and on their dreams with passion and intention, then those who have skill and experience.

As you prepare to redesign your life, keep it simple at first, so you won't feel over-whelmed. Perhaps there's one area in which you can start to live on purpose, one dream that matters to you, one project that will ignite the passion in you. Maybe it's not a project that exists yet. Maybe it's something you're going to create that comes from your heart. If you schedule it, and it matters to you, I promise that you'll have the time to do it.

Even if you are employed by a company where most of the projects you work on have been assigned, you can still find one area where you're in control, then slowly begin to work on other areas. Maybe there's a project you can bring into your company; or a project that already exists to which you're not now assigned, but which is in alignment with your interests. If you're not passionate at work, think about what quality you can bring to your job that will allow you to express more passion there. Maybe there's a piece of something you feel passionate about that you can integrate into a work project, such as your love for learning or helping others or for being creative. One man I know who has a passion for fun and baseball, turned a tedious task into a friendly, yet competitive game. He divided his colleagues into two teams, donned a referee shirt, put a whistle in his mouth and yelled, "Play ball." Which they did. A huge warehouse inventory was accomplished in record time and they all went out for beer afterwards to celebrate.

Projects are the mechanism for fulfilling your Life's Purpose.

If you can't invest your job with passion, perhaps you are turned on by an issue in your community. Follow your passion. Pursue what has heart and meaning for you.

Simplify

If you have so many things going in your life that you need to clear some out before you can get to higher ground, there's something you can do about that: simplify. Here's how.

Go back to your Purpose, the simple, broad terms of who you are, and revisit your dreams. Cross-reference that massive list of "To Dos," projects, and all the other things you've got going on, and see how they align with your dreams. Perhaps amid all that clutter there's actually something missing, an area left out of your dreams, such as having a balanced life.

Now you have another choice to make. You can add another dream, or you can take a critical look at your projects to see if you're committed to all of them. Perhaps they're not all on your "A" list. If you're compulsive about not giving anything up, and you decide that you're committed to everything, maybe there's something you don't absolutely have to do this year. Or, you may decide that it's fine to eliminate the four or five projects you feel burdened by, the ones that aren't even listed under a dream you think is important. Or you could get some help.

There is always a way to create
a life that supports who you are,
and there are always places
where things can be relaxed.

There is always a way to create a life that supports who you are, and there are always places where things can be relaxed. You can ease up in your desire to have something, your commitment to it, your schedule, or in the degree to which you need to have it. It all starts with that foundation called your Life's Purpose, the "Who are you, really?" and "Just what are you committed to?"

There are other ways to design your environment besides clearing out the clutter and finding time. I like to create a blueprint, a kind of mechanism for getting from point A to point B. In the Real People story at the end of this chapter, you will see that creating a blueprint is what we did for David, using simple imagery that will keep his commitment (literally) at hand.

Perhaps all you need to begin designing your own environment is to cut out photos from a magazine and hang them in a prominent place, as mentioned earlier. Some people like to create a Dream Board or collage, so they can keep visual images of what they want right in front of them. Maybe, like David, there's something you can develop as part of your physical self so that you can stay easily in touch with our dream and always keep it near by.

Tie things together

to simplify the journey

on the road to your dream.

Shortcuts and The Myth of Prerequisites

With his five professional areas mapped out and in front of him, David started looking for short cuts to his dream, and for short-circuits in his beliefs. His search for short-circuits was appropriate; that small voice in his head was admonishing him that he "has to do A before he could do B." Everyone has such internal dialogues: "I'll do it when I have the money, when I get the education, when my family's ready to support me, after my children are grown."

A woman once told me that she always wanted to be a doctor, but she never could amass the time or money to go to medical school.

When she got in touch with what made her feel passionate, she saw that she wanted to work in the medical field, but she didn't want to be a doctor. When she was relieved of the burdens of facing how she would go through medical school, she quickly arranged for the training she needed to become an emergency medical technician.

Sometimes people become paralyzed by the belief that, to move on, they need certain skills or additional assets. Yet there are often resources readily available to help them move quickly through the process of getting their dream. One method, of course, is skill building; another is finding or hiring somebody who has the skills to do it for you. The advice of mentors, coaches, and partners, which we discussed in chapter 12, is another great way to find a short cut.

In addition to external resources, you have, in yourself, a major resource. You can move yourself forward by being clear about what you want to do, by deciding whether your goals in one area support those in another, and by tying things together to simplify the journey on the road to your dream.

One of your most powerful

inner resources

is your own creativity.

Be willing to try on

something new

and play the game full-out.

If you're giving a speech, for example, and you tape it, you can use the tape to make other programs and to send to local radio stations. You could also try to market it or donate it to schools or libraries. You are in the best position to design your environment in ways to make your life easier. Make them up, try them on, and tie them together. Dream Big.

One of your most powerful inner resources is your own creativity, your ability to imagine and interpret. Be willing to try on something new and play the game full-out. Make requests of other people that are beyond what you thought was initially possible. Get up an hour earlier or an hour later. Flip through magazines you don't normally read. Find new ways to see things by trying on someone else's glasses, closing your eyes and finding a new perspective, going to a children's movie or a play, relaxing, using your intuition. There are many methods of breaking out of your box; you only need to look for them, experiment and try them on.

For example, there are a variety of ways to look at your current life and the resources that you already have available. We discussed some of them in chapter 11, but have you considered all the places that you frequent in the course of a week?

> your office
> your health club
> your doctor's office
> the supermarket
> movie theaters
> restaurants
> friends' homes
> the park
> coffee shops

Resources I Hadn't Previously Considered

_____

_____

_____

_____

_____

_____

_____

_____

_____

Perhaps there are resources among the people who supply you with goods or services. Maybe there's something you can tap into at your alma mater, through special courses and seminars you've attended, or teachers you've had. Think about all the cities in all the countries where you know people, or have met people in the past.

Everything in your life is a resource, most especially yourself. Examine how *you* look and speak as a resource, not just with whom you are speaking. Are you friendly and open? Do you support others' on their dreams? Are you studious? Do you have high powers of concentration? Do you go out dancing, to concerts, plays, or shows? How are you engaged with life?

What about the books you read, the videos you watch, the ideas you have, the energy you give off, even when you're dreaming in your sleep at night?   Everything that you experience is a resource you can use to design your environment. How are you using your resources?

Freedom - Letting Go

Many of us have a very basic dream that has to do with freedom. I'd love to have the freedom to do whatever I want whenever I want. Or the freedom to travel anywhere and everywhere. Or, my favorite, the freedom to shop without worrying about the cost.

However, many of us are stuck with that old belief about prerequisites—the idea that we have to do something or have something in order to be free. For a long time I wanted to move to California. I decided I'd move as soon as I could sell my Washington, D.C. condominium. Months went by, and it didn't sell. I knew that the apartment wasn't selling for a reason, that there was something for me to learn in this.

You don't have to go somewhere

in order to be free;

you can be free anywhere.

One day I pulled out my journal and asked myself, "What will I do or be in California that I'm not doing or being here and now in Washington, D.C.?" What a splendid question.

On my "Doing" list I wrote, "playing tennis, 'doing lunch,' growing my hair long, shortening my skirts, dancing, not working every day, public speaking." On my "Being" list I wrote, "playing, relaxing, listening, waking without an alarm clock, breathing, believing, and being near the water."

I began to do and be everything on my lists while I was still in D.C., and everything I wanted, to my surprise and delight, was available. That brought me to a major revelation: I could be free anywhere. I didn't have to go somewhere or do something in order to be free.

Once I had that realization, it was easy to let go of an old belief that was keeping me from the freedom I wanted, and I sold the condo. As a matter of fact, I committed to moving west before the sale, and then the sale happened.

Money Madness

Probably the most overworked excuse for not having what we want, or for not pursuing our dreams, is money, "If I only had (pick a number from $100 to $1 million) then I'd go for my dream."

My response to this is to do it anyway. Find a way to be in action. Develop alternatives. Get creative. Don't let money be what stops you.

Are you holding on
to the very thing
you want to be free of?

Find or devise the means to start now. Before I was able to sell my condo, I rented it; and if I hadn't rented it, I would have found another way. As Joseph Kennedy, Sr., said, "When the going gets tough, the tough get going."

Find yourself a different perspective. Trust me—money doesn't need to ever be the obstacle that keeps you from your dream. One couple I know is renting a magnificent home, a multi-million dollar home, paying less than two thousand dollars a month. Here's how they did it.

They saw and fell in love with a house that had been for sale and on the market for a long time. They contacted the owners and passionately described how if they lived in this home they would take great care of it. They described their dream, and how as landscapers, they would make this home even more beautiful, especially the gardens. The owner got excited about the idea, and this couple has happily been renting this mansion for almost a year. Money did not have to be what stopped them from having what they wanted, even though this dream appeared to be beyond their means.

Figure out what your belief about money is, and what your attitude is about money and your dreams. Find another "way in." Use money as a motivator or as a stepping stone, as a bridge from where you are to where you want to be.

If you hear yourself using money as an excuse, don't you believe it. There's something else going on. Check your core beliefs, change your core beliefs using the information in chapter 7, and do what you love. The money will follow. Of course, money *is* one way to gain freedom, but it's not the only way. Martin Luther King, Jr., once said he could be locked in prison and he would still be free, because freedom lived in his heart. Now, that's freedom!

What prerequisites have you put in your own way that slow you down or keep you from having your dream? Are they real? Are they necessary? Is there another way to move forward?

Real People: Judy

Judy committed to setting up all of her music paraphernalia and creating a space where she could write and sing. She reminded herself that she already was a singer by pulling out autographed photos of some of the people she had worked with years ago including The Platters and Jim Stafford. This process of gathering her momentos and bringing them back out into plain sight was a powerful step for Judy.

These images became a daily reminder of the memories that she loved and of her current dream. When she moved her keyboard in and put up a huge music banner, it instantly transformed her office space into an environment that was an expression of her passion. It was now her music room and the place where should would initiate her dream. It was from here that she made the phone call to her colleague that led to her recording session. And it only took her a day to create this space in her home.

Real People: David

David is a television and film director who wanted to do some quick "blueprinting" of the design for his life. We were having dinner at a restaurant in Los Angeles. The restaurant used paper tablecloths and made crayons available for patrons to amuse themselves while they waited for their food. David and I got into a conversation about what made him feel passionate, then we picked up some crayons and started to design David's environment. It was evident that David's purpose was to be creative.

Imagine, and explore.
Take a risk. Take a step.

He said that he was turned on by five areas of his professional life: producing, directing, editing, acting, and writing. We brainstormed to find a symbol that he could always keep with him to remind him of his five passionate dream areas. We decided to use the fingers on a hand. So we traced David's hand on the paper, wrote his name in his palm, and each one of his fingers became one of his five dreams. Imagine holding all your dreams in the palm of your hand. As soon as David felt this he had another important realization. His success in life was also in his hands.

Coming from his Purpose, David established one dream in each area that he was committed to accomplishing. Then he created three or four projects in every area, each project having specific results. David was excited about the process, and the whole year was extraordinary for him; everything he did professionally fit one of those five areas. Prior to doing the exercise, David felt he wasn't moving forward on his dream. Now he had designed and organized it in a way that made him feel powerful and get into action. Moreover, using his hand as a representation enabled David to reinforce with ease his dream and his commitment to it.

CHAPTER 15

Trusting, Timing and You

**I am not afraid of tomorrow,
for I have seen yesterday and I love today.**
— WILLIAM ALLEN WHITE

ON THE PATH TO MAKING YOUR DREAMS COME TRUE, you're going to meet up with an issue called trust. Trust, a factor that's at the core of everything, either allows your dream to manifest or keeps it from happening in your life.

I don't know any other way to build self trust then to make up a dream, put it out there in the world, give it all you've got and then, see where you wind up. Doing this repeatedly not only will help you trust yourself, but it will also build self-confidence.

What happens when you don't trust is that things get difficult, blocked, stuck or even fall apart. You start to doubt—first your decision, and eventually everything. You may start to compromise on your dream, and try to manipulate the situation. In your best attempt to control the outcome, you may be the one who unknowingly sabotages your own dream.

The key here is to notice what's going on. When you are aware of the doubts, fears, concerns, and second thoughts, you can stop for a moment and regain some clarity. Start by asking yourself "What is so." Better yet, write it out, and write out what you're thinking or telling yourself about "What is so." What stories are you making up that may be disempowering your dream? What are you not trusting and why? How can you move this obstacle, this mistrust or lack of trust out of your way? Get clear about what you don't trust and get to the bottom of it, the heart of the basic area in which you don't fully have faith in that can cost you your dream.

JUST

TRUST

Practice letting it go by being more committed to your dream and creating empowering beliefs. Ask yourself what you can do to learn trust, or to help you let go of your lack of trust.

"Letting go" happens when you have clarity about what you want, you've done everything there is to do, and now you can relax. Stop controlling, holding back, fretting or worrying. Just Trust. Two simpler words may never have been spoken; when it comes to your dream, there is nothing more profound.

Practice "Just Trust." It's a critical component for creating a life of joy and ease.

Do you trust yourself and others?

Do you trust the process, your environment, the universe, the timing, and the process?

Do you trust that your dream will come true?

What actions are you taking to demonstrate that you do trust?

Trust is a giant obstacle for many people. If you don't have it, you'll have to find it, and you'll have to practice trusting yourself above all. Trust the decisions you make, and believe that you're entitled to want your dream and to realize it. Trust comes first; that's what allows the extraordinary results to show up.

An effective exercise is to list on a piece of paper the people and things that you do trust and the things that you don't. Dan, who undertook this exercise, decided the things he trusted included himself, his wife, his minister, one of his co-workers, one of his neighbors, his mother and his brother. The things in which he didn't have faith included the people outside his immediate environment, and the natural process and timing of things. He also didn't trust that he could have a dream bigger than what already existed in his life. Writing this down brought it to he front of his awareness. From here Dan could make conscious choices to explore new options, perhaps to even practice being more trusting.

Your reality can be much bigger

than your current capacity

for dreaming about it.

Notice what you trust and what you don't. What is based on facts and reality and what might be your limiting beliefs? Just because something hasn't been done before, doesn't mean that it can't be done now.

Being Balanced

One of the ways to develop trust in yourself and the things around you is to keep yourself healthy by being centered and balanced. Feeling good about yourself leads to greater self-confidence, which is one of the places that trust comes from. You are a product of what you eat, how you live, how you rest and recreate, and what you think. All of these things filter into how you feel about yourself and, ultimately, what you allow yourself to trust.

You can work at achieving balance by incorporating some relaxation exercises into your life. The secret is to take it at your own pace, doing activities with which you feel comfortable. Take a few deep, cleansing breaths before you start a new task; closing your eyes and concentrating on your deep breathing will allow you to feel more centered. By "being here and now" you will be in touch with your life, and feeling your passion all the time. This is not about designing a five-year plan for yourself, and then spending another five years figuring out how to control your life and make it happen. It's not about having it all happen right now. It's giving yourself some flow and leeway about what you want, trusting the timing and the process, and being in action in some way each day on the things you love to do. It's really quite simple.

What I Will Do Today To Make A Difference In My Life

Starting today, I will do the following for myself:

At home: _____

_____

_____

At work: _____

_____

_____

With others: _____

_____

_____

Alone: _____

_____

_____

The element that's critical to making the timing work in your life is to be present. To be here, right now, enjoying and living your life. Take a look at what matters to you that you're not doing, being, or having. What could you change or create right now that would make a difference? You don't have to restructure your entire life this minute; maybe breathing deeply is all you need right now. Sometimes it's a matter of life or breath. Are you too busy to breathe?

Use the space on the preceding page to list the things you will start doing today. These can be simple things: taking an extra five minutes in the morning to stretch and relax, or spending 30 minutes at the end of the day reading the newspaper. Decide what you can do that will keep you centered and balanced.

In the Flow

Being in the flow means that the timing of your life is working for you, that there's a level of synchronicity where things seem to happen. One of my clients spoke to me of his dream to be featured in the local newspaper. The next day he called to tell me that the paper, seemingly out of the blue, wanted to interview him.

Surprises happen when you're living in the flow; you can get in sync with the universe when you're not so busy trying to control your life and manipulate everything. Slow down and relax, let go of some of your resistance, and things will seem to happen naturally.

Michelle decided that it was important for her business that she travel to Florida once a month, but she didn't know how she could work it into her budget. The next day a travel agency called to say that her name had been selected out of a random drawing, and that she'd won six round-trip tickets to Florida. Since then, the trips have proven so fruitful that she is considering relocating to Florida.

Yesterday I decided to hire a personal assistant. Last night, after I presented a workshop in San Francisco a young woman came up to me and said, "If you ever need a personal assistant, I would be interested in working for you." I hadn't even announced it. She starts tomorrow.

Perhaps you have some beliefs about calls that seemingly come "out of the blue." Sometimes good things happen because we have paid our dues, or because we are in the right place at the right time. Michelle's experience, winning the round-trip Florida tickets, was pure synchronicity. She had done nothing to put herself in that particular path; it just happened. I was clear about what I wanted and I believe things like this happen all the time. Maybe that's why they do.

This is by no means a trivial component of making your dream come true; letting go of the doubt and fear, and being open to greater ease, is a critical part of the process.

There are other things you can do to keep yourself centered and balanced. You can take walks in nature, go to the beach and listen to the ocean. Perhaps you will want to give yourself the gift of a extraordinary bath. Take it to the limit: light candles all over the bathroom, play soft music, pour beautiful oils in the tub, and place a bath pillow under your head. Relax, calm yourself, and retreat from worldly concerns. I know city people who go to fountains, sit close, and listen to the rushing water. For many this is the perfect time and place to dream on a whole different level.

When Life Hands You More and More

When life brings you wonderful surprises, as it inevitably will, you might begin to be concerned that you'll have too many things coming at you too fast. After all, if you enroll people in your dream, others will start trying to enroll you in theirs. As more and more possibilities become evident, how will you know when to say yes and when to say no?

Here are some simple questions you can ask yourself to determine whether or not this is right for you:

> Is this what I want to do now?

> Is this part of my dream?

> Is this something I'm passionate or excited about?

You'll know the right answer; it generally comes automatically. You'll know when you're excited about something, or when it seems like a duty. Don't be afraid to affix labels: "This is something I feel obligated to do." If that's the way you feel, you might let that project go. Other, more passion-provoking opportunities are available. In fact the possibilities are unlimited as long as you honor yourself. Follow what has heart and meaning for you. Be willing to say yes; be willing to say, "I'll think about it"; and be willing to say "no thank you!" This is an essential skill to cultivate.

The possibilities are unlimited

as long as you are

true to your Life's Purpose.

CHAPTER 16

Dare to Dream Big

**Never doubt that a small group of thoughtful,
committed citizens can change the world;
indeed it's the only thing that ever has.**
— MARGARET MEAD

SINCE PAGE 1, we've focused on you and your dream; now we're going to turn a corner. The goal of this chapter is to inspire you to dream bigger—to go beyond what you've chosen so far.

If you want to have a life that's filled with passion, I encourage you to create a project that's "Bigger Than Your Life." This project is A Big One, perhaps one you don't know how to accomplish, but one that comes from your passion.

Once you're clear about what you're committed to, incredible resources, possibilities, and people will show up to help you. Although it may not be completed during your lifetime, it will allow you to play an extraordinary game. You will definitely feel passion.

Imagine having the dream of a loving world that works, or of creating heaven on earth in your own special way. There have been many big dreamers before you—Kennedy, King, Gandhi—but there are also everyday people who absolutely can make a contribution to the world. Pursuing your Big Dream is not only about doing what you say or what you want; it's actually being and becoming a different kind of person.

**I have not the shadow of a doubt that
any man or woman can achieve what I have,
if he or she would make the same effort
and cultivate the same hope and faith.
What is faith if it is not
translated into action?**

— MAHATMA GANDHI

Where do you begin? In what area are you committed to making a difference? Are you committed to a planet that's clean and healthy? A man I know has a Big Dream to ensure that the rain forest is still in existence when his children's children are grown. Maybe your interest is in the area of health and medicine. How about a cure for cancer or AIDS in your lifetime? Or, maybe your dream, to have more breathable air, can encompass both health and environmental issues. Perhaps your contribution will be in the area of education or communications.

As I mentioned, my Big Dream is to change the way people think about dreams. I want people to stop thinking about dreams in the negative, that dreams are something they can't have. Instead, I want people to think, "Dream? By when?" and start applying dates to their dreams.

Whatever your Big Dream is, this is an opportunity for you to get into action on it. You might be asking what difference you can make if you're only one individual. The Real People stories in this chapter are about individuals and organizations that made a major contribution to society. Among them is the story of Anselm, an ordinary man who made a big difference by touching many lives globally with the projects he produced. He was only one individual, but he had a unique and special dream: to end world hunger.

If you are not the kind of person who can start a Make a Wish Foundation, perhaps you are the type who can volunteer at such an organization. Look around. Start with what you're passionate about, what matters to you, what moves you.

**We are not here to do what
has already been done.**
— ROBERT HENRI

Talk with people who are already involved and learn how you can participate. Make a contribution; that's the way to Dare to Dream Big. Make a promise and then take action to fulfill your promise; that's what your life is about.

How can you get in action? Mark your calendar; talk to someone; listen for a request; ask how you can help. As you're watching television or reading the newspaper, notice what moves you, angers you, turns you on and touches your heart. That's a good place to begin.

The critical thing is to begin. One thing will lead to another. You'll know when it feels right, and the personal feeling of satisfaction and fulfillment will be beyond description. Perhaps all we want from our lives is to make a difference. This is one way to do it: Dare to Dream Big.

Real People: Anselm Rothschild

Anselm Rothschild, a personal friend, was committed to ending hunger in the world, and he dedicated his life to doing it. He chose to pursue his dream by composing music and producing events that promoted global peace and an end to hunger.

During the 1960's, Anselm organized the Freedom from Hunger Foundation's first walkathon, which became the prototype for fundraising walkathons across the country. He didn't stop there, however. While Anselm had lots of credits and credentials, he is probably best remembered as the head writer and coordinating producer of the educational components of the *LiveAid* telecast. Anselm was a man who followed his dream. I speak about him in the past tense because, unfortunately, he died before he reached 40. But what a life he lived.

He was indeed an extraordinary man, and he wrote a wonderful song that sums up much of what I've said in this book. It's called Remember to Remember, and you will find the lyrics on the facing page.

Dreams bigger than your life
start the same
as all dreams.

Although he wasn't able to end world hunger by the time he died, his contribution made a specific and measurable difference to billions of people. Anselm's message raised awareness of the problem to a new level through *LiveAid*, which was broadcast worldwide to 160 countries.

Real People: Oprah Winfrey

Last year, I surveyed a thousand people, asking them to name Big Dreamers that they admire. The number one choice by far was Oprah Winfrey. What is it about Oprah that we love so much?

Is it that her Angel Network, where by raising over $3 million, will help pay the college tuition for kids all over the country, as well as supporting numerous other projects?

Is it her Book Club, where she demonstrates her strong belief that "education is freedom" and how she uses her television show to bring back the power, meaning and joy of the written word? Is it that she stands proudly for what she believes in?

Last week in San Francisco, I had the pleasure of giving a speech to 6000 women at the Mayor's Summit. I was on right before Oprah. As she crossed the stage, the room was transformed. We were up close and in person with an icon, a very human, kind and generous icon. It's rare when a person can bring both together, and Oprah does it with style. I think what we love most about her, is that she is real. She struggles with human frailties and emotions like the rest of us. But she courageously does it, every day in front of 30 million viewers.

Remember to Remember

Remember to remember,
It will light your heart each day,
It will help you on your way,
And it's more than just a saying so you know.

Remember to remember,
That is all you have to do,
And the truth will see you through
Even when all has darkened around you.

Who you said you are was brighter than a star,
Even though your dreams were dashed and knocked about,
You were still that dream under everything you doubt.

Remember to remember
How you said you wanted to be;
It will set and keep you free;
It will heal your wounds, caress your face with love.

Remember to remember,
If it's all you ever do,
And the truth will see you through;
You will hear God sing to you forever.

Who you said you are was brighter than a star,
Even though your dreams were dashed and knocked about,
You were still that dream under everything you doubt.

Remember to remember,
If it's all you ever do,
And the truth will see you through;
You will hear God sing to you forever.
©1989 ANSELM ROTHSCHILD

Real People: The Volunteers of the Make A Wish Foundation

The Make A Wish Foundation is a nonprofit, volunteer organization whose sole aim is to grant the wishes of children under age 18 who are suffering from life-threatening illnesses. The Foundation was started in 1980, when a dying youngster's dream to become a state trooper was granted. Since then, more than ten thousand children across the United States have had their dreams come true, thanks to the Make a Wish Foundation.

Granting a sick child's special wish provides a joyful and meaningful experience that benefits both the child and the family. Whether a child wishes to take a hot air balloon ride, visit a favorite sports hero, or spend time at Disney World, the Make a Wish Foundation does everything possible to ensure that the wish becomes a reality.

The Foundation depends completely on financial donations and on its volunteers' contributions of time. Those who elect to give of their energy are remarkable individuals, making the dreams of ailing children come true while satisfying their own desire to make a difference.

Everyday, ordinary people launch dreams

bigger than themselves .

CHAPTER 17

Preparing Your Own
Dreams-Come-True Workbook

**Before everything else, getting ready
is the secret of success.**
— HENRY FORD

OVER THE YEARS, one of the most effective vehicles I've found to ensure getting what you want is to prepare your own "Making Your Dreams
Come True® " Workbook. There is a sample Workbook at the end of this
chapter, which I have left blank so you can use it to start your own.
Use it to design and gain clarity on your most heartfelt dreams.

Don't worry about having enough time to develop your Workbook; if
you've progressed this far in the volume, you've done a lot of the work
already. Now it's a matter of setting it up in a way that will allow you
to live your dream.

You don't have to start over here; you can go back and copy the
information you need from the Passion Pyramid or any of the notes you
might have made while working through earlier chapters. Begin by filling out your Life's Purpose. Then, write the dreams you're committed to
accomplishing, and list the projects you've designed to fulfill that dream.

You will remember that, to simplify things and to make this process
really clear, you chose one area on which to focus while going through
this book. Now you have an opportunity to go back to all the dreams
under each, to list four or five different projects for each dream, with
specific results. If you haven't listed more than four or five projects,

you can list next to each project what the strategies and steps are to accomplish them.

Your Dreams Come True Workbook
will help you to set things up
in a way that will allow you
to live in your dream.

If you have a lot of projects, you can break them down even further. Thus, your completed Dreams Come True Workbook will consist of one overview sheet with your Purpose and dreams, a page for each of your dreams and its projects, and individual project sheets, listing all your strategies and steps.

When you have completed that part of your Workbook, go back through your strategies and steps and start to make notes in the margin about resources that are available to you. Maybe there's a project you're not clear about, one you can't exactly envision. Look for inspiration to clarify it. Perhaps you can see three movies in the next month that will spur creative ideas about how to accomplish that project. Even if you can't see it clearly yet, looking for inspiration is one way to be in action on a project that supports your Purpose and your dream.

Your Dreams Come True Workbook can be designed into a simple three-ring binder or in a beautiful book that you find. Break it down into the various sections: the overview, your Purpose, your dreams, your projects. However, don't be rigid about your Workbook; you may want to change its format as you go along. In any event, give yourself lots of room to expand. You will find that your initial projects turn into other projects—often more creative, challenging and rewarding—and one opportunity will lead to another. You won't know at first all the avenues that will become open to you; that's part of the magic of this process.

It's essential that you keep using any tool that you develop for getting what you want.

> **Since the mind is a specific biocomputer, it needs specific instructions and directions. The reason most people never reach their goals is that they don't define them, learn about them, or ever seriously consider them as believable or achievable. Winners can tell you where they are going, what they plan to do along the way, and who will be sharing the adventure with them.**
>
> **— DENIS WAITLEY**

That's why your Dreams Come True Workbook needs to be tied to your calendar, whether you put a calendar in your Workbook or use your Workbook side by side with your existing appointment book. Keep your Workbook someplace visible and easily accessible. Open it every day or schedule a little dreamtime. It's a way for you to reread your dream, and reconnect to your commitment. The power in doing so is that your dream exists outside of your head as well as in it; what you want is all there, with lots of clarity and room for expansion, right in front of you.

Use your Workbook also as a place for you to hold your resources. Buy the plastic sleeves available in office supply stores so that you can store news clippings or other flimsy materials. Establish sections in your Workbook for dreams you haven't yet fully developed. For example, if you want to turn a hobby into a business create a section called "My Company." If you want more bartering relationships, develop a "Bartering" section. You'll be surprised at how quickly you'll start to fill in those pages.

In the financial area of my own Workbook, I have sections for all the different ways that are available for me to make money: speaking, workshops, book sales, other products and services, investments, sponsorship opportunities. Your Workbook, in the area of personal finances, might include insurance plans, stock investments, trust funds, retirement accounts, certificates of deposit, stocks and bonds, educational funds, contributions and so forth. In any aspect of your life for which you have a project, look for ways to subdivide the components; when you do, you will find more areas of opportunity that support and reinforce you in reaching your dream.

Your Dreams Come True Workbook is

a way for you to reread your dream, and

reconnect to your commitment.

Remember, the power of your Workbook is that you will now have a place to hold your dreams. Don't be concerned that you don't know how you're going to accomplish it all or that you have blank pages; simply create the space and allow surprises and resources show up.

Making Your Dreams Come True® Workbook

YOUR NAME

WHAT IS YOUR DREAM OR THE ESSENCE OF YOUR DREAM?

_____

_____

_____

_____

_____

_____

_____

WHAT DO YOU INTEND TO ACCOMPLISH OR CREATE TODAY?

_____

_____

_____

_____

_____

_____

_____

LIST THREE MEMORIES OF PASSION:

1. _____

_____

2. _____

_____

3. _____

_____

My Life's Purpose Is:

VERSION #1

_____

_____

_____

VERSION #2 (MAKE THIS EASY TO RECALL)

_____

_____

_____

Dream Areas to Explore

MY DREAM IS TO:

Personal _____

_____

Professional _____

_____

Relationships _____

_____

Well Being _____

_____

Financial _____

_____

Fun _____

_____

Other or Outrageous _____

_____

CHECKPOINTS

Does each one "come from" your Purpose?	Yes _____	No _____
Does it line up?	Yes _____	No _____
Does this dream turn you on?	Yes _____	No _____
Are you passionate about the possibility this presents?	Yes _____	No _____

If you answered "No," change it.

Life Area: _____

_____

Dream: _____

_____

PROJECTS   **KEY**

1. _____   _____

2. _____   _____

3. _____   _____

4. _____   _____

5. _____   _____

KEY
B - Being   S - Schedule   P - Plan   D - Done

MY DREAM, ASSUMING UNLIMITED RESOURCES

Describe your dream:_____

_____

_____

Some areas to consider include: _____

_____

_____

What are you doing? _____

_____

_____

Where are you doing it? _____

_____

_____

How do you feel?_____

_____

_____

How do you look? _____

_____

_____

Who are you with?_____

_____

_____

What does your day look like? _____

_____

_____

What are you creating or accomplishing?_____

_____

_____

Give some detail._____

_____

_____

Give more detail._____

_____

ATTITUDES AND BELIEFS

Your core beliefs create your thoughts and feelings, which either empower or impede your choices and decisions. As they surface, either mentally or verbally, write your core beliefs here.

Your Attitudes & Beliefs
<create>
Your Thoughts & Feelings
<which determine>
Your Choices & Decisions

My limiting beliefs include:_____

_____

My empowering beliefs include: _____

_____

My dream is: _____

_____

The present reality about this is: _____

_____

My Limiting Attitude or Belief:_____

_____

Thought or Feeling: _____

_____

Choice or Decision: _____

_____

CHANGING YOUR BELIEF

My limiting belief that is stopping me from having my dream come true is:

_____

_____

_____

_____

My wonderful new belief is: _____

_____

_____

_____

_____

_____

MY DREAM - VERSION 2

Now what's possible? _____

_____

_____

_____

_____

_____

_____

_____

_____

Are you committed to having this dream come true?

Yes _____ No _____

Do you believe it's possible?

Yes _____ No _____

If you answered "Yes" go on; if you answered "No" go back to the
"Changing Your Belief" page.

From Dream to Project
Or
From Dream to Reality

What project can you CREATE that represents, or will get you going on, your dream?

Criterion: A project needs to be specific, measurable and have a completion date.

I recommend projects that can be done in three months or less.

Hint: You may simply add a "by when" date to your dream from the previous page.

Project: _____

_____

_____

_____

_____

_____

_____

_____

_____

Strategies and Steps
A Road Map For Getting There

STRATEGIES:

1. _____

2. _____

3. _____

4. _____

5. _____

6. _____

For Strategy #___, above, here are the steps (Items To Do) that I've chosen:

Date _____ Item _____ Resource _____

Date _____ Item _____ Resource _____

Date _____ Item _____ Resource _____

Date _____ Item _____ Resource _____

Date _____ Item _____ Resource _____

Date _____ Item _____ Resource _____

RESOURCES: THINGS I CAN DO TO HELP MAKE MY DREAM COME TRUE

Places I can go:_____

_____

_____

Things I can read: _____

_____

_____

New things I can try: _____

_____

_____

Old things I can reference: _____

_____

_____

Where is the one place I know I can't get any help?_____

_____

_____

How can I use this?_____

_____

_____

RESOURCES: PEOPLE

Friends who can help me: _____

_____

_____

Friends of friends who can help me:_____

_____

_____

Family members who can help me: _____

_____

_____

Business associates who can help me: _____

_____

_____

Organizations or Associations that can help me: _____

_____

_____

Who will support me? _____

_____

_____

Who can advise me? _____

_____

_____

Who can really help me? _____

_____

_____

People I don't know who can help me:_____

_____

_____

Who is the one person I won't get any help from? _____

_____

_____

How can I use even this? _____

_____

_____

Scheduling: Put the "items to do" in chronological order and transfer tem to your calendar.

Month_____

Day _____ To do _____

_____ _____

_____ _____

_____ _____

Month_____

Day _____ To do _____

_____ _____

_____ _____

_____ _____

Month_____

Day _____ To do _____

_____ _____

_____ _____

_____ _____

PASSION SCALE

Place an X next to the area that best describes your level of passion.

_____ RED HOT
_____ TURNED ON
_____ EXCITED
_____ VERY INTERESTED
_____ INTERESTED
_____ SOME POSSIBILITY
_____ NO INTEREST

CHAPTER 18

12 Ways to be a 21st Century Visionary

I AM HONORED to have recently been accepted into the prestigious Transformational Leadership Council. Among my peers, those who appear the most successful (and happiest) seem to be developing themselves inside and out.

My last three years have been a period of soul searching, a time of creating and a time to dream. My ego developed patience while I learned to slow down and wait for guidance. In the empty space this revelatory and relevant message emerged.

A 21st Century Visionary:

1. Has tremendous integrity. Beyond keeping their agreements with themselves and others, they answer to a higher Source. They are aligned with their values and usually have a mission, vision, calling and dreams in many areas of life.

2. Is comfortable with uncertainty, the place where true creation occurs. He or she knows we were created to create and allows the time and space for this to occur. They understand there is deep knowing under uncertainty but they appreciate the value of not knowing.

3. Has extraordinary faith. They are able to act on what's important to them even without assurance and guarantees. They can walk on faith without knowing the strategy or even clear next steps.

4. Knows that the secret to enlightenment is to relax. As we relax, our ego (with its agenda, fears and doubts) can slip away or get quiet, allowing for peace. We are left with our essential self, essence or soul.

5. Practices getting empty in order to hear the voice of the Divine

and/or feel this presence. They often create ritual and sacred space as way to invite this in.

6. Can consciously drop into a deeper place of wisdom, knowing and truth and can ideate/dream, and speak from this place.

7. Is aware that miracles happen in their own time and is able to wait rather than asserting his or her will or effort too soon. They trust the process enough to let it unfold. They can have a strong intention, yet hold it spaciously.

8. Is receptive and knows that "give and take" is not the same as "give and receive" and that giving and receiving need to be done in balance. They practice restraint, allowing space for the space where true creation and original thought happen.

9. Does not live primarily as a problem solver, but more as a creative force. They are aware that it is more powerful to move toward what you want than away from what you don't want, yet they know that both creation and destruction serve.

10. Has a conscious relationship with the silent witness, the part that can see many points of view, all sides and new perspectives. As a big dreamer, they use their imagination to traverse new terrain.

11. Knows when to be collaborative and when to be hierarchal. They have the courage, clarity and commitment to share dreams and ideas and empower others to take ownership.

12. Is crucial to the Dream Movement's ultimate dream, which is to make the world a more whole and abundant place. They know that with one single highly intentional step, the world can and has changed.

CHAPTER 19

100 Ways to Make Life Easier

I OFTEN TALK ABOUT ease as a vital concept for living a dream-come-true life. But what do I mean by "ease," and why is it important to your life and to your dreams? Designed for easy reading, here are 100 thoughts, ideas and suggestions about how to discover your passion, do more of what you love and fill your life with ease. I encourage you not to skim quickly through them, or to read them all in one sitting. Rather, treat them as you would a box of fancy chocolates: savoring each one and slowly taking in what it has to offer. As you do, you'll learn to see your life—and your dreams—in a brand-new way.

EASE: A SIMPLE CONCEPT

1. In this crazy world where life has become so over-scheduled, over-complicated and often over-critical, it's no surprise that many of us often feel defeated, or at least dazed and confused.

2. According to Webster's dictionary, "ease" means comfort and freedom from pain, worry, trouble and difficulty. Ease is about resting, relaxing and making life easier, even more natural.

3. EASE = Effortlessly Accessing and Shifting Energy. With little effort, you can tap into energy as a resource. By learning to effortlessly access and shift energy, you will come to fully understand EASE.

4. Our thoughts and emotions can cause us to burn energy efficiently or needlessly. Nervous energy makes our system work harder, while relaxing saves energy.

5. Think of ease as a way to use a small amount of energy to effort-

lessly get what you want or to change a given situation. You can do less and have more when you have ease in your life.

6. When we are out of ease, we often experience "dis-ease" and get sick. It's no surprise that being out of ease causes us to become run-down and ill. There is a direct correlation between ease and your health.

7. Learning to center offers the greatest access to ease. You are calm, not out of control, have an open mind and see what's going on. You are compassionate, able to see the other points of view, focused and available to engage with the situation.

8. In order to live a life of greater ease, one of the most important things we can learn is to meet and match our situation or our life phase with the appropriate energy. These major phases are: 1) initiation, 2) creation, 3) completion, 4) transition and 5) rest.

9. Ease has everything to do with how you use your energy to engage with life. These three techniques will empower you to take responsibility for your own life: projection, perception and point of view.

10. We have positive and negative projections. The things that you like, respect and admire in others are also true about you. Use your positive projections to learn about these parts of yourself as well.

11. Once you understand projection, you will no longer waste energy blaming, ridiculing or judging. You will shift your energy from making them or "it" wrong to demonstrating gratitude, acceptance and compassion, because you will see that what you are upset about and reacting to is *you*.

12. How we view the world, other people and the messes we get ourselves into is important. How we choose to clean them up is essential. To practice ease, practice being responsible for your perceptions and actions.

13. Willingness to see a new point of view can completely shift the energy and resolve tension. When we take a fixed position, we may ultimately lose what matters to us. Being flexible will always give you much more range than rigidity.

14. Shifting your point of view gives you access to more options

and an opportunity to grow. It helps you get to the heart of the matter and to stop wasting energy, which is what ease is all about.

THE ULTIMATE DREAM: A LIFE OF EASE

15. What determines how much ease you will have is how you deal with life. If what you seek is more joy, juice and jubilation, you have to let it in. The ideal way to experience a life of ease is to meet life open-armed, open-minded and, most important, open-hearted.

16. If you create dreams or goals that you are more committed to than your reality, which includes your worries and doubts, and if you do something to move your dreams forward daily, you will transform your life.

17. Doing less is not about doing nothing. It is about center and balance. It is about choice and freedom. And it is about getting rid of garbage: old beliefs and emotional baggage that is weighing you down.

18. Your "having more" list may actually turn into your "having less" list, as you purge and clear out the clutter.

19. The death of a habitual behavior is required to allow new life, energy and ideas in. Although it may be difficult to imagine at this point, surrendering some control actually leads to greater self-trust, confidence and ease.

20. Trust is developed by trusting. It comes as we surrender, and as we surrender, we learn to trust that we will survive. Surrender comes with practice. The great reward for deep surrender is often complete change. The world can literally be seen from a new perspective.

21. It takes letting go of what we know to access a deeper place of wisdom and to expand our capacity. Having a broader repertoire of life skills to choose from provides less frustration, more choices and ultimately greater ease.

22. One of the most important tools to develop and utilize is the power of your will. By being clear about what you want or need and being open to what life may bring you, will and intention blend together into a magnificent moving force.

23. It is possible to use will without resistance, without judgment and without effort. It can be used to manifest what you want through a laser-like focusing process. Get highly intentional, focus on what you want, and there it is.

24. You will actually create more by honoring what matters to you most. Doing what you love will give you more energy, enthusiasm, vitality and happiness.

25. Don't write off these techniques as being overly simple or trite. It is how you use what you know and learn that allows you to develop yourself as a master. Transformation can happen in a day, even in a moment.

MAKING LIFE "EASE"-Y

26. Different situations at different times in life obviously require different responses. Practice, inquire and experiment. Ask yourself, "Where do I need to go inside myself emotionally or physically? What will give me ease right now?"

27. Schedule an EASE break. The purpose of this break is to rest, and to access and shift your energy. It is in this quiet time that some of the most profound things can happen.

28. Breathing is by far the best way to access energy and put ease in your life. It helps us dissolve stress and feel more alive and connected to ourselves, others and life. It helps remove emotional blocks and burdensome thoughts. Breathing is guaranteed to shift your energy.

29. Doing nothing is a skill that most of us aren't very good at or comfortable with because we never cultivated it. If you are interested in ease, the skill of waiting is worth pursuing.

30. While you are in the decision-making process regarding anything important in your life, it is not time to act. But spend too much time deciding and you may dissipate your energy or miss the opportunity.

31. Taking action links vision and passion because as your imaginative juices get sparked, your projects get charged and energized. This will intensify the creative process, further inspiring you to keep going.

32. So much is possible just through talking. You can articulate

your point of view or express an idea; you can ask for feedback, or share a feeling or an experience.

33. Dreams connect the unconscious to the conscious. When you are asleep, your mind is free to roam. You can receive guidance and knowledge. Learning to work with your dreams gives you access to your own unbounded creativity.

34. Our feelings can be powerful messengers, but often we are either cut off from them or swept away by them. If you can be in tune with what you are feeling, you will have access to a deep and wise part of yourself.

35. As a powerful tool for shifting energy, laughter is in a category by itself, and it is highly underused.

36. Movement is one of the most direct and powerful ways to get your energy moving. It's not a mental process, so you don't have to figure anything out or need to understand how it works. You just have to bring your body and show up.

37. To talk to you about ease, shifting energy or doing less without discussing meditation is impossible. When our mind is still, empty and quiet, we can totally relax, and this also relaxes the body. After meditating, even just for twenty minutes, you will feel refreshed.

38. There are patterns and symbols that offer insight and understanding, wisdom and knowledge. Use them to deepen your awareness and understanding and to grow and try new things.

39. If you can clearly see where you are and know where you want to be, figuring out how to get there actually is easy.

THE TEST OF EASE

40. The secret to doing less and having more is awareness. Come to know who you are and how you deal with life's annoyances and inconveniences. Then try some new options.

41. Since awareness is such an essential part of creating ease in your life, it's useful to recognize where you lose ease and become stressed.

42. As you become more aware, you will gain greater skill at ac-

cessing ease. You may try new ways of responding to those daily occurrences that can make us all a little crazy.

43. As you come to recognize your style, you become more self-aware. The more conscious we become about how we react, the more willing and able we are to try other things to achieve ease.

44. The game here is not to change who you are or to get rid of your defective parts. The goal is to broaden and expand, learn and integrate. Come to know all of yourself.

45. All those nagging behaviors that I didn't like about other people are just unintegrated and disowned parts of myself. Nothing will give us greater ease than recognizing and accepting our differences.

46. There is a wise guide that lives in each of us. It is the part of you that remains calm in chaos. It is even the part of you that can see both sides of an argument. It is your witness.

47. The witness, also known as the aware ego, is something you should seek to develop. As you observe your feelings and reactions, you will begin to notice patterns of behavior. You will have more access to *you*.

48. Doing less and having more is about options, exploring alternative behaviors and learning to see things from new perspectives. Explore where you might like to expand your range or simply try something new.

49. Use everything for your growth and development. Learn about you, learn about others, and of course, learn about life.

THE EASE OF KNOWING YOURSELF

50. What will give you ease is to know yourself, to determine your own belief system and to live by your own convictions. Have your beliefs and opinions, be open to input and see things anew. Have the courage to disagree with something that seems invalid or to dismiss something that seems unnecessary.

51. If you are not clear about what you want, it's impossible for anyone else to know either. Vagueness sends conflicting messages and makes it hard for others to help you. Vagueness and confusion start an

entire downward-spiral process, often leading to self-doubt and a sense of futility.

52. Make decisions in a timely fashion. Only you can decide what that is. Put all the facts down on paper, listing the "pros and cons" or writing out all your concerns and fears.

53. Notice when you are reacting without checking in, and practice taking more time to evaluate your needs.

54. When we understand why we operate the way we do, we'll have some choice about what serves us best in any given situation.

55. Be aware of behaviors or pursuits that perhaps have outgrown their usefulness or effectiveness. Habitual behaviors are sometimes hard to spot. When a habit is starting to cost you something, especially your creativity or sense of play, it's time to re-evaluate.

56. Self-reflection and contemplation can be nurturing, calming and clearing, but when it comes to simplifying your life, other people are not only useful, but often are essential.

57. If you are suspicious that some part or all of your life is now in a rut, consider asking a friend or family member about it. Others often see things about us that we are blind to. If you are hearing the same feedback often, say three times or more, take a good hard look at what's being said.

58. If you believe everything you're told, you will get confused. For every yes, there is a no. For everyone who thinks your ideas are mad or wild, there is someone who will think you are clever and brilliant.

59. There are some things in life we have control over and many that we don't. The way in which you meet life will determine the amount of ease and grace you have in your life. Change what you can, release what is not needed, accept what you are able to accept and get into relationship with the rest of it.

60. If we take half the energy we use to moan, groan and complain and direct it into achieving our hopes and desires, our lives will look completely different.

61. With a dream you can design a strategy or a plan to make it

happen; with a fantasy, you cannot. Just because it's a fantasy doesn't mean it can't or won't happen. But there is little you can do that will make it happen.

62. Setting yourself up for failure by embracing a fantasy is self-defeating. If you are seeking something, define what it is, where it can be found and who can help you.

63. Often we know what we need to do, or what the next step is, but we don't take it. Inactivity keeps you stuck, and the way to get unstuck is to do something. Taking action changes everything.

THE ROADMAP TO EASE

64. Once you are clear about your passion, purpose and dream, and armed with a strong belief, the Roadmap to Ease is where it all becomes real.

65. The key to this process will be your passion. The purpose of the roadmap is to connect you to what you love, inspire you and encourage you to live the life of your dreams.

66. When it comes to ease, one of the most common problems is that we treat our life as though it were a big pot of soup. We throw everything into one big pot and then wonder why it tastes so bland or awful.

67. In any given pot are our passions, dreams and limiting beliefs. If you want greater ease in your life, if you want to do less and have more, we need to see what's in your soup.

68. As you start to feel your dreams and desires, your limiting beliefs will show up. And as you start to act on what you truly want, reality will test you.

69. Until we know who we are and what really moves us, is impossible to truly know our deepest dreams and desires.

70. Often we are so wrapped up in reality that we have forgotten our dreams. Without our dreams, all we have is reality. Although reality is not a bad thing, you are living a different kind of life when you are focused only on reality than you would be if you were also pursuing your dreams.

71. Some of us are good at dreaming and being creative, but per-

haps are lacking in the implementation phase. Or perhaps you need some practice or work in the dreaming or imagining aspects of life, but are quite skilled at planning to meet your goals.

72. Each step you take in creating your dream life will move you closer to that life. A great hint for success is to try to do something, at least one tip, technique or exercise, each day. These are not cumbersome and they will keep you motivated.

73. Look for success. Find one thing that you did today that made you feel positive. Notice where you did less. See where you had more. Acknowledge your successes and modify your behaviors as you go.

74. Armed with simple but effective techniques, people do magnificent and exciting things. By following the roadmap to ease, and using passion, dreams, beliefs, tasks and teams, you too will experience a shift in your world.

YOUR PERSONAL PROFILE

75. What will give you the greatest ease of all is to know yourself—your personal needs and timing, your hopes and desires, your doubts and concerns—and to honor these.

76. How you begin each day, and the practices you follow throughout the day, can help or hinder you. There's tremendous power in developing daily rituals and practices. Learn what works for you and incorporate this into your day.

77. Discovering your personal daily rhythm and "prime-time" is a simple awareness tool that can be really helpful in reclaiming your life and having more ease.

78. In order to have ease in your life, you need to take care of yourself. Pay attention to the essential basics. When we are healthy, wealthy and wise often follow.

79. Develop your own Internal Tracking System (ITS). Learn to recognize what you need, at the moment you need it, for more immediate ease in your life. When your ITS says it's hungry, eat; when it's thirsty, drink; when it's tired, sleep or rest.

80. When I want one final comprehensive check on how I feel about something or my level of interest, I take my Passion Pulse. I rate my level of excitement, joy or enthusiasm. I know that passion and commitment go hand in hand, so I don't treat this response lightly.

81. By testing my level of passion, I am really checking out my level of intent and willingness for serious participation. Life is just too short to keep saying "yes" when what's in your heart is "no."

82. Imagine what would make your life easier and more joyful. The key here is to keep it simple. Just adding one thing to your life, something you will commit to doing daily for one week, will begin to build awareness.

83. Even when you're extremely pressed for time, you can access ease. Whether you are stressed out over a decision, running late to an event or in "overwhelm mode," help is instantly available by taking a breath.

84. When an opportunity presents itself, ask yourself one very clear question: "Will this make my life easier?"

85. Explore being of service and contributing to others, which builds self-esteem and a very full life. If risk-taking is fun for you, schedule an adventure or two.

86. When life becomes overwhelming, or if a crisis is throwing you for a loop, take a Personal Pause. Rather than doing or saying something you may regret, take a little time to check in, reflect and consider your options. The very act of pausing can be life-changing.

87. Doing less and having more is all about designing your life. You can directly impact the way you live.

88. Do more of what you love, when you love to do it. Do less of what you don't like, or do it when you can get it done quickly. Ultimate ease is finding what works for you and wherever you can, bringing it into your daily life.

STEPS FOR ONGOING EASE

89. Life will test us. Life will keep us busy and too often distracted.

When life shows up with all its distractions and annoyances, as well as its opportunities and rewards, you can be ready with your ease tools.

90. When something happens that throws you "off center," follow this six-step formula: *Recognize* what's happening when it happens. *Realize* and *reflect* on what you are doing and where or how you have done this before. Get into *relationship* with the people and situation involved. *Respond* and *re-create* the scenario.

91. The idea behind this maintenance program is to easily incorporate these steps into your existing repertoire so you can easily practice ease on a daily basis, and especially during stressful times.

92. Just noticing or realizing what's happening, when it's happening, is a life-changing skill that you already possess. Soon you will find yourself automatically much more relaxed and have a much greater capacity to deal with challenging situations.

93. Realization begins with stopping. Stop and notice what you are feeling. As you realize what's happening, as it is happening, you can begin to use life's encounters as a resource for growth and to have ease in your life.

94. To realize something is not just to see it, or have a thought about it, but to feel the emotions associated with these thoughts, and, when necessary, to take appropriate action.

95. To realize something is to give yourself the potential to shift it, or at least to shift your relationship to it. For what you once could not see, hear, recognize or understand now exists in your conscious awareness, to be examined and understood.

96. It is the ongoing practice of asking and answering questions and acting on what you think, believe and know that will deepen your intuition, instincts and risk-taking abilities.

97. Practice minimizing stress around important decisions by exploring options and deepening your self-trust. Think new thoughts, try new ways and recognize what works. These are essential tools for building the kind of life you want.

98. Without inspiration, we would expire or die. Taking care of some

of your needs and recognizing and realizing some of your own dreams is essential. Talking about your dreams and passions is not a frivolous conversation. It inspires you and has everything to do with ease.

99. As we reveal ourselves and see others, we can heal and grow and become more whole. True love is not a destination, not a place to get to or a goal to obtain. Love is about bringing wholeness forward.

100. Until we begin to recognize and realize that we are more than we can see or touch, until we begin to feel our feelings and relate to ourselves, we will not know true inner peace. And without inner peace, ease is impossible.

CHAPTER 20

100 More Ways to Make Life Easier

"SUMMERTIME, AND THE LIVIN' IS EASY…" That old, slow Gershwin standard conjures up images of sipping lemonade in a hammock on a sultry summer afternoon, doesn't it? But that kind of "easy living" isn't quite what I have in mind when I encourage you to learn to live a life of ease. The "ease" I'm talking about will aid you in bringing purpose, happiness and satisfaction into your life. Here are 100 truths and suggestions for living a passionate life filled with ease, ideas that you can use as you take action to make your dreams come true.

PASSION: THE JUICE

1. If you want to do less and have more, identifying your passion is important.

2. Passion can give us energy to handle the things that overwhelm us. When you are in touch with your passion, you have more energy, vitality and creativity.

3. The happiest people know that passion lives inside of them and the secret to a fulfilling life is to find ways to consciously design more of what they love into their everyday existence.

4. Begin to recognize who you are passionate about *being* rather than just what are you passionate about *doing*. Why? Because the broader your area of passion, the more places you can express it.

5. For some, taking what you love and turning it into a vocation would kill the passion. For others, being paid for doing what you love would be the ultimate dream come true.

6. Once you know your passion, you can actively design the life you

want and put more passion and vitality into your life, regardless of what you are doing, where you are doing it or who you are doing it with.

7. Live "on purpose" by designing a blueprint for achieving what you want and you will streamline the process of reaching your dreams.

8. If what you want is to live life fully, have fun and wonderful relationships at work and at home, and ultimately make your dreams come true, it is essential that you explore your purpose.

9. Passion is the access to ease, and the way to tap your passion is through your life's purpose. Your purpose is who you are or what gets you excited. I might even say that your purpose is remembering why you're here.

10. Start with your purpose and rest assured that you will accomplish things faster and easier when you are passionate and "on purpose."

11. Standing in your purpose, you will be able to develop projects that will take your dreams out of your imagination and make them part of your reality. Not only will your projects be "real," but they will further the journey toward realizing your dreams.

12. By taking the time to define your purpose, you'll open up more time and space, have more energy, and be more focused. Life becomes richer and has personal meaning.

13. When you have a sense of your passion and purpose, you have the ability to be responsible for your own happiness and satisfaction, both at home and on the job.

14. Once you have established your foundation and know who you are, you can start to look at how you want your life to be.

DREAMS: THE FOCUS

15. A dream is defined as a fervent hope or desire. Making your dreams come true is about getting clear about what you want and figuring out how to obtain it. The prime dream we are working to achieve here is doing less and having more.

16. Goal-setting is important, but there's a different kind of energy released around dreams. Our dreams are spacious and creative. You

don't need to know how to make a dream happen, you don't have to believe it's possible and you never actually have to do anything about your dreams.

17. The formula for getting what you want is: get clear about your dream; remove the obstacles to your dream, especially the limiting beliefs; and design the strategies for achieving your dream.

18. Write your dream down. Do not omit this step. Don't fool yourself by saying you know what it is. Write it down so it is out of your head and you can see it.

19. The talking process is useful because it can help your dream grow and crystallize. It is in the expression of what we love that we actually begin to see it and create it. Talk your heart out.

20. Great things happen when we share our dreams with others. It is essential that the people in your life know you are committed to greater ease. And if they don't support your dream, you definitely need to know that, and find someone who does.

21. The strategy for making any dream come true is creating a clear dream, breaking it down into small steps, identifying the resources that can help, and taking action every day.

22. Here are six different ways or places where you can access dreams: Expression, inspiration, real-life desires, active imagination, sleeping and exploration.

23. If there's something simple that can be brought into your life right now that will make you feel good and give you ease, do it. Make an investment in yourself and bring part of your dream into reality. You will be that much closer to having it all.

24. Start by thinking about your dream as being real, by visualizing it and expanding on your image. Learn to speak about it clearly; the more you speak about it, the more detailed it will become.

25. Your nocturnal dreams offer exceptional communications and deserve special time for closer examination. Treat them with respect and reverence, honor them as teachers, and they will reward you justly.

26. I can't stress enough the importance of making an honest as-

sessment of where you are now. Starting with inaccurate information will lead to erroneous decisions about what has to be done and how far you have to go to reach your dream.

27. In order to create a life of ease, where you are doing less and having more, it is essential that you are more committed to your dream than to your reality.

28. Without your dreams, all you have is reality, and although this is not a bad thing, there is a very different kind of energy attained from your dreams than from going through life checking things off your task list. Taking action for the sole purpose of getting rid of a problem usually leads us back to the problem.

BELIEFS: THE FOUNDATION

29. In the early stages of creating a dream, there isn't always evidence that your idea is a good one, or that this is the right time to launch it. The same is true about a big dream, like doing less and having more.

30. Your beliefs become the necessary foundation to support you in moving forward in your new life. Since our attitudes and beliefs determine the choices and decisions we make, your beliefs will either empower you or impede you.

31. Your beliefs are never neutral. They either move you forward or hold you back. Our attitudes and beliefs determine our thoughts and feelings. These shape our choices and decisions.

32. Being aware of your beliefs is the first step toward changing them. When we can hear the subtle conversations in our head, we have some power over them. It's the unconscious limiting beliefs that often sabotage us or catch us off guard.

33. Consider my acronym for the word BUT: Believe, Understand, Trust. Use the BUT theory to keep your beliefs optimistic and your dreams alive and well.

34. This process of reframing how you deal with objections can change your outlook on life and support you in taking risks. If we be-

lieve in our dreams, we tend to move forward; if we don't, we tend to be stagnant or complacent.

35. You have plenty of opportunities to practice accessing your new belief, shifting the downward spiral of doubt and putting you back in touch with what you want.

36. Confidence means to confide in yourself. Self-trust comes from practice. It is a skill that can be honed and it is essential for creating greater ease.

37. Our beliefs are our own opinions and judgments, but for some strange reason we seem to forget that we can choose them. In any given moment and in any given circumstance, we choose what we believe.

38. When you are not consciously choosing to believe an empowering belief, what you get by default is your old limiting beliefs. Choose a belief that will empower your dreams for having greater ease, for doing less and having more.

39. What does it take to change a limiting belief to a positive belief? It takes willingness, choice and practice. Be willing to choose a new belief and practice believing it by acting on it.

40. At the bottom of all our excuses, the fear of failing keeps us immobilized. Our fear is natural and understandable. But if we don't learn to use it or interface with it, it will keep us stuck.

41. Even fear can serve a purpose. We do not need to be stopped by it. In fact, we can even be motivated by it.

42. Don't do your dream in. Don't let your ego sabotage your goals with doubts, fears and concerns. When these come up, ask yourself this ever-empowering question: "What am I more committed to, my dream or my reality?"

43. If you are not acting on your dream, you are acting on your fears and beliefs. Although change always brings up all sorts of doubts and concerns, it's how you deal with them that matters.

TASKS: THE MOMENTUM

44. Dreams die when we put them on our "To Do" list. They are too big, overwhelming and unmanageable. The way to achieve big dreams is to create small projects.

45. A project or goal is often defined as a dream with a deadline. Projects make our dreams real. Dream first, then set goals for the dreams you want to move forward.

46. Tasks are the essential tools needed to create what you want. Although at first you may consider tasks to be arduous work and more responsibility, the proper use of them can be transformational.

47. Create a project, or several projects, that can easily be accomplished in three months or less, since short-term projects help us see quick results. Each project should be specific and measurable and have a due date.

48. A project can deal with any aspect of your life. When you pursue projects, you are mastering the techniques of consciously designing your entire life. You can only learn these by practicing.

49. To make your project part of your reality, you will need strategies and tasks to guide you toward your dream. A strategy is the approach you take to achieve your dream.

50. Tasks are the specific steps needed to accomplish the strategy. An entire project may include several strategies, each comprised of several tasks. If the separate tasks aren't listed individually, the project usually never happens.

51. The single steps that you take every day toward your dream determine the quality of your life. Our goal is to have these tasks, as much as possible, be things that you enjoy and that move you toward your dream.

52. Use your passion as your guide in saying "no thank you" to the tasks you can decline, and you will have more time and space in your life. As you lessen what you don't want and don't need, and increase what you love and want, your life will be changed.

53. As long as your projects come from your purpose and are aligned

with your dreams, as long as you still feel the passion, stay in action. If you still feel the passion, stay in action.

54. Projects come in all sizes and shapes. Begin with a project that will fulfill your dream of having greater ease in your life. When you are ready, perhaps now or sometime in the future, design other projects that excite and have meaning for you.

55. No project is too small. The only criterion is that you be passionate about it.

EASE TEAMS: THE SUPPORT

56. The number-one way to experience ease in your life is to share your dreams with others and ask for help. The best way I know to do this is to build "Ease Teams."

57. I know what you are thinking. "I will not share my dream because people might laugh at me, think I'm lazy or crazy, steal my idea, or—here's the biggie—they might expect me to do something about it."

58. The problem is that unless you are sharing your dreams, they remain a secret. And often, an unspoken dream is forgotten.

59. Identify people who share your dream of having greater ease. This could be your Ease Team. Whether it is people in your family, at work, in the community, or even strangers, when you team up with other like-minded people you can find ways to share resources, as well as inspire each other.

60. It's your prime Ease Team that will truly make the difference in your daily life. These are the people you know you can count on to help you, support you and even hold you accountable to your vision. These people are resources you need to make your life easier.

61. What's essential in the beginning of this process is that you find at least one other person who believes in the dream and is willing to support you. The strength of the team grows exponentially if the interest is mutual.

62. Create a robust database. Make sure your own fabulous resources are only a phone call away.

63. The job of your travel Ease Team should be to make your life easier and, ideally, to make your travel experience a pleasant one. If you travel a lot and don't have this team in place, I strongly recommend that you create it now.

64. Communication is an essential strategy for any project. Talk to the people in your life, even the negative people. Find out what they are thinking and feeling. Give them some space to have their concerns and reactions.

65. Break your dream down into projects with due dates. This will help you identify exactly what you need and where you can use some assistance.

66. Most of us enjoy making a contribution or being supportive, but we are busy and overwhelmed. If you can make it uncomplicated for people to respond affirmatively to you, you will have mastered a powerful skill for having greater ease.

67. What is essential for doing less and having more is to build an extraordinary team of people around you. Find people you trust, people you can count on. Then honor these relationships as gold.

MOMENT BY MOMENT

68. Without a doubt, the single biggest contributor to stress, or lack of ease in our life, is time. How we spend it, use it and perhaps waste it has become a problem of epidemic proportions.

69. We must learn to shift our relationship to time. This is something we absolutely can do. We can make the most out of time by actually experiencing life as opposed to doing as much as we possibly can.

70. When we shift our relationship to time, we shift our relationship to life and how we live. Stress and anxiety about time occur when we relate more to the future than to the present.

71. Time management doesn't give us more time. Although it speeds up the treadmill and we may become more productive, we're only doing more. Time management may worsen our stress because we're not actually shifting our relationship to time.

72. You can loosen technology's grip on your life by using your fax

machine, e-mail, voice mail and pager only when necessary or when you choose to. Take control of your time by learning not to answer immediately.

73. We need to find our own rhythm, our own flow. By becoming aware of your natural rhythm, of your internal clock, you can begin to create and shift your relationship to time. You can begin to use time as a gift for creating ease.

74. In the present moment there actually is no stress. Stress comes in our resistance to this present moment. If you could just relax into it, allowing this precious moment to be whatever it is, it would be a priceless gift.

75. Is this you? "I am forever questioning where I am and wishing I was elsewhere, when all I really need to do for ease is to get still, get present and realize that where I am is the perfect place to be."

76. We can take back our lives in small ways. Small steps build confidence to take larger leaps. Less stress means more success and more time and energy for the people and things you love.

77. Learn to infuse the spirit of ease into everything you do in everyday life by cultivating awareness.

78. Spontaneity, in moderation, can give you a breather, reignite your passion and give you a new perspective. Give spontaneity a shot.

79. Passion can be the ultimate time-saving tool for two good reasons. First, when you are doing what you love, who cares about the time? Second, when you are doing what you love, it often gets done faster than when you are doing only the things you need to do.

THE COMPLETION CORNER

80. Complete what you start, when you start it, even if part of the completion process is to decide not to do it anymore. Keep your mind relaxed and available for the things that matter to you. You will find this a life-changing practice.

81. The more honest you can be with yourself, the more powerful this process will be. And the more detached you can stay from the procedure, the less painful it will be. Don't judge or belittle yourself because some part of your life is in disarray.

82. Clarity about where you are helps shine a bright spotlight on what needs to be done, created or accomplished. Remember, our goal here is to clear out the clutter, emotionally and physically, and make plenty of room for ease and flow.

83. Completion creates freedom. Having a sense of humor and keeping a sense of lightness about this process is useful. Your goal is completion and ease, not an obsessive compulsion.

84. When you're not looking over your shoulder at all the incompletions in your life, you can be focused on moving ahead. When your energy isn't diffused or wasted in a fixing or fretting mode, you are available to play.

85. Keeping your word is how you show yourself that you are accountable. You demonstrate to yourself that your word is powerful because you honor what you say. You use it to create, and it works.

86. The more your life is in order, the faster and easier your ability to manifest will become. You'll find that almost as soon as you say what you want or ask for what you need, it shows up.

87. Let's not disregard the power of chaos as a force for change. Let's honor and respect the energy behind a creative whirlwind. Let's be open to order *and* chaos, welcoming and practicing both!

88. There are two common experiences associated with completing. One is fulfilment and satisfaction. The other is depression and loss. Both come up often when we undertake a creative endeavor.

89. If you have fear completing, reread the section on beliefs. Format a powerful belief that will help move you out of your fear. Fear of completing can be energy-draining and can kill the dreamer inside of you.

90. Completing is just as important as beginning. Begin, do or express, complete, and begin again.

EASE IN REAL LIFE

91. As you begin to develop your skills for having greater ease, life will offer you many opportunities for practice and perfection.

92. Do not panic, have an unnecessary big reaction, lose your cool, blame or attack, or make matters worse. Remain calm in the midst of chaos. This is what ease is about.

93. Get into relationship with the people who can bring ease, and with it great happiness, into your life.

94. The most successful people use their passion to engage others, or use it to influence and make changes.

95. What I love about real wisdom is it's so simple. There are wonderful ways you can do less and have more, no matter where you are, who you are with or what you are doing.

96. Hard work won't kill you, but smart work is easier. Working smart requires you deal with challenging situations and includes planning.

97. In life, you can do everything "right," but through events beyond your control, everything can still go wrong. You have to learn to deal with it and just let it go. When we stop getting upset about or trying to control situations that are out of our hands, we are practicing surrender and ease.

98. Strive for balance. When we do not balance our activities for any extended period of time, everything seems to fall apart. Learn to make time for all the things that matter to you. A successful life includes work time, family time, self time and spiritual time.

99. Moment by moment is the only way we can live life. Savor life and you'll understand the true joy of doing less and having more, every precious instant of every priceless day.

100. No matter where we are or what we are doing, life provides wonderful opportunities and lessons. To push and resist is to learn the hard way. If we remain open, centered and available to the lessons life is handing us, we experience ease.

CHAPTER 21

Useful Words for Making Dreams Come True

To speak of "mere words" is much like speaking of "mere dynamite."
— C.J. DUCASSE

THE FOLLOWING WORDS AND DEFINITIONS, as used in this book, are also used regularly by people who make their dreams come true. Think of these terms as a new way of speaking your dream. Hear yourself use them and know yourself as a Dreamer.

Accomplishment, something that you have done, succeeded in, or completed in the past that you are proud of; something that you're passionate about.

Acknowledge, to recognize or to be proud of.

Action, to move from one point to another; to be in motion; a dynamic movement forward.

Alignment, when everything is arranged in a way that works and supports the whole.

Balance, equal on all sides; the outcome is a sense of well-being and ease.

Belief, an assumption you have; a way of looking at things that determines your choices.

Clarity, focus; a clear way of seeing something.

Coach, a person who is committed to your being a champion.

Completion, when something is whole; has integrity; all the pieces are there.

Conversation, a way of communicating and interacting with another person.

Design, to make something happen intentionally.

Devise, to plan; a plan of action.

Dream, a fond hope and a plan for accomplishing it.

Dream Architect, someone who helps other people accomplish their dreams by helping them get clear about what they want, by helping them to design a blueprint for achieving their dreams, and by helping them make their dreams come true.

Dynamic, an energetic force that is intense, exuberant, unstoppable, in motion, full speed ahead, moving forward.

Energy, a force; a potential; the ability to move.

Enrollment, sharing your dream in such a way that other people get excited.

Expressing, a way of communicating; conversing, relating, telling, declaring, imparting information to others.

Focus, an ability to see things clearly using different perspectives.

Fun, amusement, mirth, gaiety.

Happy, lightness, enjoyment, pleasurable, feeling good.

Harmony, when all things work together in unison.

Intention, focus; direction.

Love, a way of being; that which has deep meaning and significance for you.

Measurable, something that can be evaluated using preset criteria.

Movement, relocation of something from one place to another.

Opportunities, the variety of ways of accomplishing something.

Participation, involvement; making something happen.

Partnership, relationships with people who can help you make your dreams come true.

Passion, feeling turned on, energized, excited enthusiastic; going full out, aligning mind, body, heart.

Play, to engage in, undertake, perform.

Possibility, the belief that anything and everything can happen; a powerful force.

Power, a form of energy, such as owning your own power; energetic movement from A to B; also a form of empowerment.

Projects, a unit of measure for accomplishing something; an accomplishment with a specific, measurable result; the way to bring your dreams into tangible form.

Purpose, who you are in the world; work that you have chosen to do in the world; where passion comes from; what turns you on.

Relationships, a way of being with another person or other people or things.

Resources, tools that are available to help you make your dreams come true, including people, places, things, and you.

Result, an accomplishment; something complete and whole that stands alone; something that can be identified and measured.

Scheme, a plan of action.

Schedule, to put something on your calendar; to assign a date by which something will happen.

Specific, an individual unit that is identifiable in time and space.

Steps, that which moves you forward.

Strategy, a way of doing something; the "how" of getting something accomplished.

Success, a self-defined way of being, the outcome of which is a feeling of joy.

Tactics, the specific items to get you into action on making your dream come true.

Unlimited, no restrictions or limitations on what you want to accomplish.

Unstoppable, to keep going, no matter what happens.

Values, a way of being; a way of living your life.

Vision, a clear picture of what you want to accomplish or create.

Vitality, a level of energy and usefulness that one may have when living life on purpose.

Way of Being, the expression of someone living their life in passion.

Way of Living, unlimited; no restrictions; anything goes.

Whole, something that is, or someone that is, complete and intact and has all the pieces.

Work, an expression of who you are in the world.

CHAPTER 22

Epilogue:
The Beginning

We can create and live the life of our dreams.
Wake up and dream.
— MARCIA WIEDER

ALTHOUGH THIS IS THE LAST CHAPTER of the book, it is only the beginning for you. Remember your dreams are the expression of your heart and soul. Get in touch with what matters to you most. Bring more of who and what you love in to your every day life. This is your life and although life is short, it is how we live it, each and every day, that will make it joyful and fulfilling.

Remember that the formula for Making Your Dreams Come True® is:

1. Get clear about what you want to create,
2. Remove the obstacles, and
3. Design the simple steps to make your dreams happen.

And of course, keep in mind the shortcut step is to share your dreams with others. Build DreamTeams. Ask people to join your team and ask how you can help them achieve their dreams.

Standing in your Purpose and moving up the Passion Pyramid, you can see your dreams in crystal clarity and commit to having them. Use your resources, the ones you know about right now and the ones you can make available to yourself. Allow yourself to be imaginative and inventive, to create projects that will move you forward.

Design your internal and external environments so that they are nurturing to your dreams and to the projects that will make your dreams come true. Trust the process, the synchronicity in the universe and, most of all, trust yourself. You are, and you can be, as imaginative and resourceful as you need to be; get in action to live the life you love. Remember, you are a dreamer at heart.

Share your dream with others; the process will help you enroll people who will want to contribute time and energy to fulfilling your dream. When you can envision it in its entirety, you will be able to speak about your dream in a way that generates excitement and enthusiasm. The eagerness you engender in others will come back to you a thousand-fold in heightened motivation to make your dreams come true.

Be unstoppable. You can have the life you want, the one that works for you. The possibilities are all waiting for you to let them happen, to produce extraordinary results, to make your life the magical experience it was meant to be.

About the author

MARCIA WIEDER, CEO/FOUNDER OF DREAM UNIVERSITY® is leading a Dream Movement. With over twenty years coaching, training and speaking experience, her inspiring message, style and wit has touched audiences from 50-5,000 at companies such as AT&T, The Gap and American Express.

Whether teaching at the Stanford Business School, speaking to executives in China, or addressing young women at Girl Scout Camp, her riveting style impacts audiences world-wide. She is the personal Dream Coach to Jack Canfield, stars in Beyond the Secret with Bob Proctor and is a member of the prestigious Transformational Leadership Council along with John Gray and Marianne Williamson.

As past president of the National Association of Women Business Owners, she was often in the White house where she met former U.S. presidents, Ronald Reagan, Jimmy Carter and George Bush Sr. And as a columnist for The San Francisco Chronicle, she urged readers to take "The Great Dream Challenge."

Marcia has appeared several times on Oprah, The Today show, in her own PBS-TV special and has written 14 books that have been translated into numerous languages. Her newest is called *Dreams are Whispers from the Soul*.

She lives in Mill Valley, California where she is pursuing her dream of living near the water, balancing work and play, with much more emphasis on play.

Marcia Wieder
Speaker/Author

MARCIA GIVES SPEECHES AND PRESENTS inspiring workshops on dream achievement, team building and visionary thinking. Her most requested titles include:

> Igniting Passion in Your Work & Life

> Big Dreamers: The Secrets of Leaders & Top Performers

> The Business of Making Dreams Come True

> 12 Ways to Be a 21st Century Leader & Visionary

> Secrets of Big Dreamers & High Achievers

> Create Your Dream Life: On Your Way in Just One Day

> Visionary Women: Outrageous, Outlandish and Just Like You

If you would like to know more, please call: 415-381-5564
Or visit our website: **www.MarciaWieder.com**

Dream University®

DREAM UNIVERSITY® is the only university in the world solely dedicated to helping you discover and achieve your personal and professional dreams. Our results-oriented courses, inspiring faculty, supportive community, and networking alumni offer practical resources to take action toward success on your own terms.

Dream University® has an online campus in order to fulfill its mission to teach millions of people worldwide how to achieve their dreams. Regardless of your location or socioeconomic status, DreamU will provide you with its proven methods, tools and world class faculty to help you identify and achieve your dreams.

Dream University® is for you if:
> You want to create and realize an important personal or professional dream.
> You desire new clarity and resources for the 21st century.
> You want to express your voice as a visionary or leader.
> You dare to dream big!

Live Events include:
> Create Your Future Now Workshop
> Design an Inspired Life
> Dream Coach® Certification
> The Spiritual Leader Workshop
> Masterful Workshop Conductor
> Become an Inspiring Speaker

Visit: **www.DreamUniversity.com**

Thank you for Being a Fellow Dreamer

Here's a Gift for You –
Three beautiful e-books designed to help you dream big and succeed.
Feel free to share them with friends and family.
www.DreamUniversity.com/gift